TWELVE YEARS WITH MARY BAKER EDDY

RECOLLECTIONS AND EXPERIENCES

Irving C. Tomlinson

Twelve Years
with
Mary Baker Eddy

—

RECOLLECTIONS AND EXPERIENCES

—

REV. IRVING C. TOMLINSON, M.A., C.S.B.

The Christian Science Publishing Society
Boston, Massachusetts, U. S. A.

PUBLISHER'S NOTE

Reverend Irving C. Tomlinson, M. A., C. S. B., the author of this book, was born in Perry, New York, the son of the Reverend Dewitt Clinton and Emmeline C. Eaton Tomlinson. Early in life Mr. Tomlinson's steps were directed along religious lines. In the year 1880, he was graduated from Akron University, Akron, Ohio, with the degree of Bachelor of Arts, and in 1883 he received the degree of Master of Arts. Five years later, he was graduated as a Bachelor of Divinity from the Theological Department of Tufts College, in Medford, Massachusetts. For several years following his graduation, he served as a Universalist clergyman in the vicinity of Boston.

Christian Science first came to Mr. Tomlinson's attention in 1894. Within three years he joined The Mother Church, The First Church of Christ, Scientist, in Boston, Massachusetts, where he later served as President on two different occasions. He was a practitioner, teacher, and lecturer of Christian Science for many years. He taught the Normal class of the Christian Science Board of Education in 1928. In addition, he was engaged in various other activities of the movement. For twelve years he was closely associated with Mary Baker Eddy, the Discoverer and Founder of Christian Science, and from 1908 until 1910, as one of her secretaries, he was a member of her household at Chestnut Hill.

During the years of his close association with Mrs.

Eddy, Mr. Tomlinson kept an account of certain incidents as they occurred. This record supplies much of the interesting material in this book, and refers solely to the life and work of the Leader of the Christian Science movement.

Wherever Mrs. Eddy's spoken words are recorded, the author has given them as accurately as his memory permitted, but it is well to bear in mind that it is the sentiment which is expressed rather than her exact words.

ILLUSTRATIONS

FOREWORD

CLARA CLEMENS, in her biography "My Husband Gabrilowitsch," quotes the following remarks made by her father, the world-famous humorist Mark Twain, concerning Mary Baker Eddy, the Discoverer and Founder of Christian Science:

> Christian Science is humanity's boon. . . . She [Mrs. Eddy] has organized and made available a healing principle that for two thousand years has never been employed except as the merest kind of guess-work. She is the benefactor of the age.[1]

As the years advance, the world is coming more and more to agree with Mark Twain's estimate and to recognize that Mrs. Eddy's discovery of Christian Science denotes a distinct turning point in human history.

It is therefore beyond question that any authentic, firsthand information regarding the author of "Science and Health with Key to the Scriptures" is of absorbing interest, not only to Christian Scientists, but to all thoughtful people. And it is the realization of this ever-growing interest in the Discoverer and Founder of Christian Science that has prompted me to prepare this volume based on my recollections and experiences.

This book is intended to be exactly what its title represents, the record of my years with Mrs. Eddy, and although it includes biographical material dealing with Mrs. Eddy (some of it never before published), it is

[1] Used by permission of Harper & Brothers.

distinctly not intended to be merely another biography. Mrs. Eddy's own book "Retrospection and Introspection" gives her human history. Her life record has been dealt with in the following authorized publications: "The Life of Mary Baker Eddy" by Sibyl Wilbur, "Mary Baker Eddy: A Life Size Portrait" by Dr. Lyman P. Powell, "Christian Science and Its Discoverer" by E. Mary Ramsay, "Historical Sketches" by Clifford P. Smith, and "A Child's Life of Mary Baker Eddy" by Ella H. Hay.

These recollections deal with the period of twelve years (1898–1910), when I had the joyful opportunity of serving Mrs. Eddy and the Cause of Christian Science in various capacities and during part of which time I was one of her secretaries and a member of her household. These were some of the most active and productive years of Mrs. Eddy's life.

While living at Chestnut Hill,[1] it was my blessed privilege (in common with other members of the household) to see Mrs. Eddy almost daily, to receive instructions from her, and to hear her explain innumerable details connected with her manifold labors. Many of the experiences related were shared by others. Many of them were simply my own.

Sometimes when we were all gathered together, Mrs. Eddy would discuss with us passages from the Bible which she had just been reading. Frequently she would question us on some Scriptural text and after listening to our replies would give us spiritual interpretations that would completely illumine the Bible references. On other

[1] Mrs. Eddy's residence in Newton, Massachusetts.

occasions, Mrs. Eddy would recall some incident from her childhood days and with twinkling eyes humorously describe the people, the surroundings, and all the circumstances pertaining to the occurrence. Then at other times, with the most loving expression on her face, Mrs. Eddy would tell us of some of her early healings or perhaps recall some instance of her mother's tender love or present some illustration of her brother Albert's extraordinary ability.

During the years of my association with Mrs. Eddy I kept an account of events at the time they took place. As soon as I conveniently could, I wrote down as accurately as I was able to remember them Mrs. Eddy's words spoken in conversation or instruction when the household was gathered in her study, or during quiet talks when I was alone with her. Many of the remarkable things she said and did which are included in this book are taken from my impressions which I had recorded and from some of the numerous letters Mrs. Eddy wrote to me. It was also my privilege to read Mrs. Eddy's own scrapbook and to receive her permission to make extracts from it.

My years of service with Mrs. Eddy and the Cause began in 1898, and it may be of interest to the reader to retrace briefly the steps that led up to that ever-memorable period.

After graduation from Akron University in Ohio, I took the divinity course at Tufts College, Medford, at the conclusion of which I immediately entered into the ministry of the Universalist Church. It was while pastor of the First Universalist Church of Arlington, Massachusetts, that I had an interesting experience which proved to be the direct cause of my eventually becoming a Christian Scientist. One of my parishioners was a victim of the drinking habit, and in an effort to help him I persuaded him to undergo a popular materia medica treatment of that day known as the Keeley Cure. For a time, at least, the man appeared to receive some benefit and I was lauded to the skies by members of my congregation for the splendid part I had played in the matter. As a matter of fact, I did not think it was "splendid" at all and the praise I received embarrassed me, for my own inability to heal the man seemed most unsatisfactory to one who was supposed to be a follower of the Master. One night during this experience I turned to my Bible for enlightenment and in the sixteenth chapter of Mark I came across these words: "And these signs shall follow them that believe; In my name shall they cast out devils; they shall speak with new tongues; they shall take up serpents; and if they drink any deadly thing, it shall not hurt them; they shall lay hands on the sick, and they shall recover."

I began to ponder this passage as I never had before. Jesus' command was unmistakable, yet all I had been able to do to help a poor victim of alcohol was to recommend the Keeley Cure. I then began to wonder if there was any church that attempted to do the healing work our Master bade us perform. Next morning I began calling on clergymen of various denominations to find an answer to my question, but my visits proved fruitless. It was not until eleven months later, in 1894, that I

"I attended my first Christian Science service in Chickering Hall"

received a completely satisfying answer to my question when I attended my first Christian Science service in Chickering Hall, Boston. Further help came in 1895, when I paid my first visit to the original Mother Church, The First Church of Christ, Scientist, in Boston, Massachusetts.

It was a Sunday service I attended and, oddly enough, in the foyer I met a former member of my own church, who kindly invited me to share his pew.[1] It will amuse Christian Scientists (as it now amuses me) to recall that at the conclusion of the service I remarked to my friend with the arrogance of ignorance: "You'll never be able to hold this congregation with that kind of service, a man and a woman reading. What you need is a magnetic personality in the pulpit." My friend replied: "A year ago we had eight hundred in the congregation. Now we have twelve hundred." I had no adequate reply.

I then began attending the Friday[2] evening meetings and heard testimonies of healings that convinced me that there was at least one church carrying out the Master's injunction to heal the sick. I thereupon began to make a sincere investigation of Christian Science and had the good fortune to meet Mrs. Flavia S. Knapp, C. S. D., wife of Mr. Ira O. Knapp (member of the first Board of Directors of The Mother Church), who took a kindly interest in my desire to know more of Christian Science. Some time later I applied to Mrs. Knapp for permission to become a member of her class and Mrs. Knapp wrote

[1] The Mother Church at that time had rented pews.
[2] The Wednesday evening meetings were formerly held on Friday evenings.

to Mrs. Eddy for guidance. She graciously gave her consent for Mrs. Knapp to include me in the class, although at the time I was still a Universalist minister in good standing. In fact I was still preaching in the Universalist church, and on the Sunday before Mrs. Knapp's class was ended I took a copy of Mrs. Eddy's textbook, "Science and Health with Key to the Scriptures," into the pulpit with me at Lynn and read from the chapter on "Prayer" to my somewhat astonished congregation. As a direct result of this reading, one of the church members who was ill at the time was prompted to seek a Christian Science practitioner for treatment and received a healing. But the gentlemen who comprised the Fellowship Committee of my church were not favorably impressed with my innovation and politely but firmly requested me not to read any more from what they called Mrs. Eddy's "Bible."

Not long after Mrs. Knapp's class ended, I resigned from the Universalist church. By then I had found it impossible to ride two horses going in opposite directions. In 1897, I became a member of The Mother Church and in that same year entered into the practice of Christian Science. In 1898, Mrs. Eddy made me a member of the Bible Lesson Committee, where I served almost continuously for over twenty years. Also in 1898, she appointed me a member of the Board of Lectureship, and I had the honor of delivering the first lecture on Christian Science ever given by a member of that Board. In November of that same memorable year I had the unbounded privilege to be a member of the last class Mrs. Eddy ever taught.

And in December she invited my sister and me to visit her at Pleasant View, Concord, New Hampshire.

I shall never forget that visit or Mrs. Eddy's graciousness and consideration. She expressed such tender, loving, motherly solicitude that I was instantly drawn to her.

Like everyone else who has ever come into our Leader's presence, I was impressed with the soulful quality of her deep-set blue eyes. They seemed to look right through me on that memorable visit.

Mrs. Eddy was slight in form, and although not above average height, she bore herself with such stately dignity that she appeared much taller than she actually was. In her conversation she displayed the keenest intelligence and a thorough grasp of whatever subject she was discussing, and I was amazed at her energy, originality, and executive ability.

I was well aware that I was in the presence of a remarkable and noble woman, one who had, without human aid, revolutionized the spiritual thinking of a world, organized a church, and reintroduced the Christ-healing that had been lost for nineteen centuries. Yet, in the interests of truth, I have to record that in spite of all these facts I did not at that time recognize Mary Baker Eddy (as I later did) for what she really was—God's messenger to this age!

It was during this visit that Mrs. Eddy invited me and my sister Mary to become First and Second Readers of the Concord church, positions we held, by Mrs. Eddy's request, for seven years.

From that time on I was privileged to serve our Leader

at Concord in different capacities until January 26, 1908, at which time she left for Chestnut Hill. Here I was a member of her household as long as she remained with us, which was until December, 1910.

As one who enjoyed the priceless privilege of service with Mary Baker Eddy, the Discoverer and Founder of Christian Science, I know that her every waking hour was dedicated to the worship of God and the welfare of man. In Mrs. Eddy's calendar there were no periods of respite from active duty. Every member of her household knew that she never passed one moment in idleness. Her days were spent in unselfed labor, her only rest that which comes from righteous activity. Strengthened by the ever-presence of divine Love, she was sustained throughout her labors.

Mary Baker Eddy's self-effacement was so complete that her love for God and man was the ruling motive of her existence; and that motive illumined her life with increasing beauty and power as the years advanced. Her own words epitomize her life: "My private life is given to a servitude the fruit of which all mankind may share."[1]

Mrs. Eddy in her own daily activities exemplified the beautiful passage regarding the Master which she gives on page 25 of Science and Health: "The divinity of the Christ was made manifest in the humanity of Jesus."

I shall forever be indebted to Mary Baker Eddy for her tender, wise words of counsel and admonition, for her love, inspiration, and unselfish example. And I value as priceless privileges each duty assigned, each task ful-

[1] Miscellany, p. 218.

[8]

filled, that came to me at the behest of that great woman.

It is with the most profound gratitude that these pages are presented in the hope that others may share some of the blessings that were mine for twelve glorious years of inspired association with the Discoverer and Founder of Christian Science, Mary Baker Eddy.

These pages record the truth of her own words which she modestly wrote me in a letter which now appears in Miscellany (p. 247): "The little that I have accomplished has all been done through love,—self-forgetful, patient, unfaltering tenderness."

THE AUTHOR

CHAPTER I

IT has often been said with truth as well as wit that New England is really a state of mind rather than a geographical designation! The very name New England connotes certain qualities and characteristics of a distinctly individual nature that through the centuries have never ceased to be expressive of its earliest settlers.

When we mentally visualize a New Englander we think instinctively of one endowed with the pioneer spirit, rugged individuality, granite courage, simplicity, perseverance and, above all, a spiritual devoutness that may sometimes be tinged with a certain austerity.

In the finest sense of the term, Mary Baker Eddy was indeed a true daughter of New England, typifying in her character a combination of its grandest qualities. And for her to manifest the pioneer spirit throughout her life was entirely natural, for her heritage was a guarantee of that spirit.

Mrs. Eddy with good reason regarded highly her early ancestors and their pioneer history. Her forefathers were among the early settlers of New England and to know them was to know a group of truly independent thinkers. The founder of the family and the first to sail from England to the New World was John Baker, who, in 1634, settled in Charlestown, Massachusetts. Records show that John Baker's family and descendants could always be found laboring to uphold the free institutions of America, particularly a free ballot, a free press, a free school, and a free church. In common with nearly all those early New England settlers, the Baker family, even amidst the rigors of pioneer life, Indian attacks, severe climatic conditions, and an inhospitable soil, paid strict attention to their religious faith and made the worship of God first among their daily duties.

On her mother's side of the family Mrs. Eddy's grandfather, Deacon Nathaniel Ambrose of Pembroke, was mainly responsible for the erection of the North Congregational Meeting House. In view of Mrs. Eddy's achievements in establishing her own church it is interesting to learn that on both sides of her family her grandparents were instrumental in establishing churches; the Ambroses giving substantially of time and money to a Congregational church and the Bakers to a Methodist church. And so generous were their contributions and so faithful their service that these two churches were known as the Ambrose and the Baker Meeting Houses. It was not the nature of the Bakers or the Ambroses to follow in the rut of others' spiritual beliefs. They sought the inspired truth for themselves and once they were convinced of its divine source they unfalteringly took their stand. To do God's will was the cornerstone of their purpose in life. And Mrs. Eddy's parents maintained the great tradition of the Baker and Ambrose families in placing service to God above all other considerations. And so, logically and inevitably, it was in an atmosphere highly conducive to spiritual unfoldment and devout living that the child of Mark and Abigail Baker was born on July 16, 1821, at Bow, New Hampshire.

Both Mark and Abigail Baker were deeply religious, and many a time in later years Mrs. Eddy loved to recall her mother's devotion to the church and her constant study of the Scriptures. Mrs. Eddy always spoke in the tenderest terms of those early years of loving association with her mother and all that they had meant in her life. She often said that it was her mother who had encouraged her in her devotion to the Bible and the realization of God's ever-present love.

As Mrs. Eddy related, time and again, incidents of her childhood days on the farm at Bow, the members of her household were amazed at her powers of remembrance. She readily recalled not only names and dates but conversations. Sermons and lectures which she had listened to as a child she remembered distinctly and repeated them with an astonishing clearness of detail.

Mrs. Eddy never ceased to hold the dearest memories of her old home, and one day, accompanied by one of her students, she paid a visit to her birthplace. Following the back road and coming to the top of the hill overlooking the farm, she beheld once more the spot where as a child she had played with her brothers and sisters. Tears came to her eyes as she gazed on the old familiar scene and saw the field where her childhood home still stood.

Always of a tender, loving nature toward every living thing, Mary's affectionate solicitude was excited by the animals on the farm. Often at night, tucked in her warm bed, the child could not go to sleep if she heard the distant squealing of little pigs in the farmyard. She would rise, run down to the pen and sing to the pigs until her father came after her, gathered her up in his arms and put her back to bed. Young lambs were her special care. "Here is another invalid for Mary," her father would say as he brought in a weakling of the flock, and Mary would patiently watch over the little creature and nurse it back to health.

It was natural for Mary to think of others before herself. In the fall she would go off into the woods with the other children after chestnuts, and on returning home her father would say, "Who pities father?" and Mary would instantly give him every nut she had gathered. "You need not give away all you have, Mary," cautioned her mother. "You know the Bible says, 'Love thy neighbour as thyself.' It does not say, 'Love thy neighbor better than thyself,' for justice belongs to both."

This spirit of giving and sharing permeated the very fiber of her being. She was the living embodiment of the Scriptural precept, "It is more blessed to give than to receive." Little Mary Baker often gave away her mittens, her cap, and even her warm coat to some poor, shivering child at school less fortunate than herself. She just could not bear to witness any kind of distress without doing something to remove it.

"My child, you must not give away your clothes today," her mother would say as she dressed Mary for school. "Mother has not time to make others for you, and you have given away so much it is not right to ask father to do more for you." That desire to give never left Mrs. Eddy, and throughout her life she continued to bestow without thought of self the riches of her love and generosity wherever she saw a need.

In and out of season Mary was always the champion of the weak and oppressed. In the school at Bow there was an older girl who played the tyrant over the smaller children and was such a young terror that even the boys feared her. She made the lives of others so miserable that little Mary resolved to do something about it. One day the older girl brought a hollowed-out cucumber to school and filled it with muddy water taken from the side of the road. Entering the schoolroom with the cucumber held aloft, she sent the little tots huddling in terror to the far end of the room. "Now," she cried, "every one of you must take a drink from the cucumber." Recalling this incident in after years, Mrs. Eddy said, as I remember:

I can see her now as she started down the aisle toward the terrified scholars. I could not have been more than eight years of age, but I planted myself in the aisle down which she was coming and exclaimed, "You shall not touch one of them. I will not permit it."

But the girl tossed her head and cried, "Out of my way or I will knock you over." I folded my arms and stood my ground with the words, "No, you will not lay a finger on me nor harm one of them."

She paused, looked at me, laid the cucumber down and remarked, "You are a brave little rascal." Throwing her arms around me she kissed me. Thereafter whenever she went to impose upon the children I went to the rescue and prevented her from doing harm until she gave up all attempts to annoy or injure the weaker ones. The teacher confessed to me that I had done what whipping had failed to do, for I had completely changed her character.

In that small village school was a child that no one seemed to care for. No one played with her. No one paid any attention to her. As soon as Mary realized the situation she invited the unhappy little girl to a seat opposite her own and showed her such kindness and friendliness that the other children grew ashamed of their cruel treatment. Later in life, when that lonely child had become a happy wife and mother, she met Mrs. Eddy and reminded her of her kindness in that schoolroom of long ago, a kindness she said that had had an influence for good on her entire future.

Mary's father, Mark Baker, was a man of stern but righteous convictions, a staunch supporter of austere Calvinistic doctrine. He was held in such high esteem by his friends and neighbors that he was frequently called upon to defend them in the courts, on one occasion having as opposing counsel Franklin Pierce, later President of the United States. Although lawyer Pierce presented his case with that resourcefulness and ability which afterward gained him the chief honor at the hands of his fellow countrymen, the case was decided in favor of the people's advocate, "Mark Baker, the lay lawyer of Bow," as Mr. Baker was then designated.

Firm in his adherence to whatever he considered his duty, Mark Baker conducted religious services daily in the home, which included a reading from the Bible and long, long prayers.

On one occasion Mary listened (from her trundle bed) while her father and her grown-up cousin, Aaron Baker, debated long into the night over the doctrines of Universalism. It seems that Cousin Aaron had been dipping into the writings of Hosea Ballou, whose unorthodox opinions troubled Mary's father considerably, and he felt it was his duty to pray long and earnestly with his nephew, fearing that Aaron's soul might be lost and cast into utter darkness. In any case, that little child Mary again and again stayed wide-awake throughout long religious discussions, joined in daily prayers, and listened eagerly for every word she could catch that referred to the Bible, the prophets, the Master and his disciples.

One evening, tucked in bed, when she was only eight years old, Mary listened to a discussion over a Bible text that lasted for a solid three hours. When, many years later, Mrs. Eddy mentioned this incident to her household, someone asked her if she had not grown sleepy. Mrs. Eddy replied in substance:

Never—I always wanted to know who won. It was always my joy to listen to a sermon or to hear a discussion upon a Bible subject. After hearing it, I would go over it again and again and pray over it far into the night. Even in my childhood days, I would much rather study the Bible or listen to a discussion of it than to go out to play with the children. After school I would seat myself in the rocker, and while I rocked read the Psalms of David or the life of the Master. At twelve years of age my dear Book of books was well thumbed and worn, and many of my favorite Psalms and whole chapters of the New Testament I could repeat by heart.

Speaking of her childhood experiences at the supper table one evening, Mrs. Eddy, according to my recollection, gave us the following illuminating picture of her father:

The great old Bible on the stand was my grandsire's wedding gift. The devotions in our home were solemn moments. Morning and evening we had the long prayers and a chapter from the Bible —and the prayer was a long one. Often too long for my short little limbs, seated as I was on a bench.

At mealtimes, we had grace before the meal, and returning of thanks after every meal, and these prayers were not always short, either. Nor did it matter how threatening was the storm and how many tons of hay were in the field—father never permitted the order of these devotions to be altered in any particular.

"Did your mother ever talk in these services?" someone asked, and she replied substantially as follows:

Never. Women were then expected to keep silent and to yield place to their masters. But mother prayed much alone and was a deep student of her Bible.

I have never seen one who had such a gift of audible prayer as my father. Appropriate passages of Scriptures flowed from his lips in boundless measure, and his earnestness and zeal in prayer were, to my knowledge, without parallel.

On Sunday, the entire family attended the forenoon and the afternoon services, and the children were not allowed to go elsewhere than to church—not even to the cemetery. Father kept the family in the tightest harness I have ever known. When my sisters were having young gentlemen callers, he would step to the door and say, "Let all conversation and pleasure be in harmony with the will of God."

Although Mary was a loving and obedient child, church customs and ceremonies sometimes puzzled and confused the tiny head. Mrs. Eddy smiled as she told us of her early attendance at a Communion service. Her account was somewhat as follows:

There being no Congregational church in Bow after the year 1829, my parents attended either the old North Church in Concord, or the church which my grandfather, Nathaniel Ambrose, built in Pembroke, just across the Merrimac River.

One Communion Sunday when I was a very little girl, we attended this sacred sanctuary. It was the first Communion I had ever attended, and when the bread was passed I took a piece and commenced to eat it. My dear mother took hold of my arm and tried to shake the bread from my hand, but I held on tightly and would not loosen my grasp until the beloved one took it from my fingers.

The tears streamed down my cheeks, but I bore my grief in silence. At the conclusion of the service, mother told me I must not do so again. "But," I said, "I was hungry and wanted something to eat."

Mrs. Eddy had unbounded love and a great respect for her brother Albert. On one occasion in talking of him she said in effect:

At the time Albert entered the New Hampshire legislature, he was tall and commanding in appearance. He possessed the manners of a Chesterfield and manifested the tenderness of a woman. He had a massive head, a high, projecting forehead, dark auburn hair, and clear brown eyes that expressed intelligence and love.

When he entered the legislature a visitor who saw him for the first time asked if he were not Andrew Jackson.

My brother had a beautiful tenor voice and people would come miles to hear him sing. I remember his singing in crowded parlors and one song especially, "Comin' Thro' the Rye," was a favorite. His voice is as clear in my memory now as when I heard him singing in those olden days.

Speaking of his rare abilities and keen sense of justice in connection with his activities in behalf of the people of New Hampshire, she said, as I remember:

He was instrumental in having placed upon the statutes a law relating to the poor debtors. A venerable aged gentleman, highly respected for his long years of business integrity, met with sudden reverses and was cast into prison as a poor debtor. Albert valiantly attacked this unjust law, and was successful in obtaining the repeal. Never again in the history of the Commonwealth was a respected citizen cast into prison for debt.

By invitation of Franklin Pierce, Albert became a member of his law firm.

In addition to the companionship Mrs. Eddy always enjoyed with her brother in her early years, she also found in her sister Abigail a loving friend and faithful confidante. But unfortunately, later in life, Abigail Tilton never understood her sister's spiritual discovery and consequently had no use for Christian Science.

As her delicate physical condition for many years prevented a regular attendance at the Bow schools, Mary Baker received much of her early instruction from her parents, who, needless to say, saw to it that the child's moral and spiritual training were properly attended to. When Mary did go to school, her brother George, who was very fond of his sister, used to walk nearly a mile to meet her so that he could carry her home on his shoulder and thus conserve her strength.

At an early age Mary had the good fortune to receive academic instruction from her brother Albert, who took a great deal of interest in her education. He set about tutoring her systematically in order that his little sister might know "something more each day than the day before," specializing in English and in languages, including Greek, Latin, and Hebrew.

When she was able to attend school, Mary's quick perception and keen understanding received high praise from her instructors. One time during a lesson in philosophy the teacher asked the class this question: "If you were to take an orange, throw away the peel, squeeze out the juice, destroy the seeds and pulp, what would be left?" Many said they did not know. Some said that nothing would remain, while others kept silent. But when the question was put to Mary she replied, "There would be left the *thought* of the orange."

At an early age Mary Baker showed decided ability as a writer. And her literary gifts received not only encouragement but exactly the right kind of direction when at school she came under the tutelage of Miss Sarah Jane Bodwell, daughter of the Reverend Abraham Bodwell, for many years pastor of the Congregational Church at Sanbornton Square. In telling us of her experiences Mrs. Eddy said that it was a most thorough training she received, not surpassed even by our colleges of today.

Although it was customary for each pupil to hand in an essay once a week, Mary sometimes arrived at school without having prepared one. But before school was over she would have one completed, having written it at odd moments during the day. Astonished at this rapid production of a well-written composition, her teacher once said to her, "Mary, some day you will be a distinguished author!"—a prophecy that indeed came true.

Mrs. Eddy's schooling was considerably in advance of that received by the average girl of her day, the Sanbornton Academy standards being well above those of most of the institutions available for girls at that period. She also attended Holmes Academy at Plymouth, New

Hampshire. It must be remembered that there were very few higher institutions of learning for women then in existence, and the men's universities had not even dreamt of opening their exclusive doors to women. In the days of Mrs. Eddy's youth a young woman certainly had to make a considerable effort of her own if she wished to acquire an education.

Mary Baker took full advantage of every form of instruction that was available, whether at school or under the guidance of her brother Albert. In proof of this, it is interesting to note that long before her discovery of Christian Science Mrs. Eddy was a steady contributor to magazines and newspapers. For a time she earned a substantial income from her writings, but after 1866 she gave up everything in order to devote her whole time to her great lifework which was then just beginning.

From infancy Mary Baker was a brilliant, original, affectionate but frail child, experiencing frequent periods of illness. She enjoyed few of the activities of normal childhood, but devoted herself to her studies, particularly to those of a spiritual nature. Her early occupation with the things of the spirit was a fitting preparation for the great task she was later destined to fulfill. It was her love for God and her fellow man that had filled her consciousness from infancy which, later in life, helped to sustain her through every ordeal and provided that strength from within that so frequently astonished all who knew her.

In 1843, Mary Baker, now grown to young womanhood, married Major George W. Glover and sailed with her husband for Charleston, South Carolina. Her brother George, a close friend of Major Glover, played a considerable part in furthering the attachment between his sister and his friend. Mrs. Eddy told her household one evening the story of her meeting Major Glover and their friendship, which was substantially as follows:

When my brother was married, Major George W. Glover, my future husband, was present at the wedding. I was so timid that I would not come into the room during the ceremony.

He asked me at that time to correspond with him, and in this way we got acquainted, for in writing to him I became very fond of him. My father did not wish me to write to Major Glover, for he feared it would end in marriage.

For a long time I received no letters. My brother George, who loved me dearly, declared that father took the letters. So he said, "Mary, you shall go with me to the mountains for three weeks or more, where I am sure you will get the letters." He wrote Major Glover, and true enough when we got to the mountains I received my letters regularly. Major Glover said that he had written me every week as he had promised, but my father had burned the letters. Our hired boy Lyman had gone for the mail and had given the letters to my father.

My brother George said, "Mary, I have investigated and have found Major Glover a fine man. He has a good business and will make you a good husband."

Not long after, Major Glover returned and we were married Sunday morning by the clergyman, in my father's parlor. It was not that my father disliked Major Glover that he did not want me to marry him, but father did not want me to go so far away from home.

With this marriage a great sense of happiness had come into the life of the frail, earnest young woman of the New Hampshire hills. But it was destined to last only a short while.

Major George W. Glover

CHAPTER II

THE young wife of Major Glover, who accompanied her husband to her new home in South Carolina, soon gave evidence that she was the same Mary Baker of New England, whose deep-rooted love of freedom and hatred of injustice still burned within her with unquenchable intensity.

A change of residence from North to South in no way affected Mary Baker's inner self.

At the time of her arrival in the South, the plantation owners were absorbed in the management of their estates. Social life, lavish entertainment, and the enjoyment of leisure occupied much of their time. In the pleasure-loving atmosphere of the pre-Civil War South, Mary Baker found many friends and much that was beautiful, but the question of slavery constantly confronted her.

Slavery was repulsive to one of Mary Baker's tender, loving nature. Strongly in favor of abolition while living in the North, she became even more definitely convinced of the evils of slavery now that she found herself in its stronghold. When she spoke with her husband about it, he, thoroughly impregnated with the Southern viewpoint, scarcely understood her. Patiently he explained to her that it would be economically disastrous to free slaves, since the whole industrial system of the South was founded upon slavery. In fact, as he endeavored to make clear to her, it was not possible to free them, for South Carolina had forbidden it by statute passed in 1820. Nevertheless, Major Glover's young wife protested against the system which, inherently, she felt to be wrong. Looking back to that faraway period, Mrs. Eddy once spoke to me of her deep convictions, which I recall as follows:

Even while in the South I did all I could to teach and preach abolition, although it brought protests from my dear husband. I began the education of our servants. I spoke freely against slavery and wrote vigorous articles for the press in favor of freedom. This created such opposition that my husband came to me and said that, although he had many friends, he did not know that their friendship would save me, should it become known that I was the advocate of freeing slaves. I persevered, however, in my endeavors to benefit the bondmen, although the antagonism became so intense that placards were posted threatening destruction to the abolitionist.

It is a pleasure to recall the keen interest which Mrs. Eddy manifested when she showed me her letter to General Benjamin F. Butler, thanking him for his noble stand in behalf of the colored race.

Rumney, N. H., August 17, 1861.

General Benjamin F. Butler

My dear Sir:—

Permit me individually, and as the representative of thousands of my sex in your native state, to tender the homage and gratitude due to you, one of her noblest sons, who so bravely vindicated the claims of humanity in your late letter to Secretary Cameron. You dared to assume, in the dignity of defending with your latest breath our country's honor, a position of justice and equity. The final solution of the great National query,—Will freedom be rendered to black as well as white—men, women, and children—whom you have the courage and honor to defend in this hour of our country's pain and purification?—must soon follow.

You hold freedom to be the normal condition of those made in God's image: so do we all. In this, the man can only equal the soldier who offers his life for his country, and by fairness of argument elucidates the justice which will surely transmit to posterity the success of a republican form of government, in heritage perpetual, undimmed in its lustre. The red strife between right and wrong will be fierce, but it cannot be long, and victory on the side of immutable justice will be well worth its cost.

. . . Your act has thrilled with electric hope the homes and hearts of this section of our country,—hope in God and in the Right. Give us in the field and on the forum men like our brave Ben. Butler, and our country is saved.

Respectfully,

Mary M. Patterson [Eddy].

In his appreciative response to Mrs. Eddy's words of gratitude, General Butler was pleased to say, "The discharge of public duty is made easy by such commendation, coming from the noble and the loyal of the land."

Mary Baker's sojourn in the South was not destined to be of long duration, for after a few brief months of happy companionship Major Glover passed on. He had taken his young wife with him on a business trip to Wilmington, North Carolina, where he was stricken with yellow fever and passed away within nine days.

Major Glover was deeply mourned by his many friends, who manifested a tender sympathy for his young widow. In telling me of the many kindnesses of her friends, Mrs. Eddy especially recalled the loving attention of the rector of the Episcopal church which she and her husband had attended. I remember that she also said:

Another strong helper was Thomas D. Mears, a member of a prominent North Carolina family. One day soon after Major

[25]

Glover's passing, he asked me to step with him into an adjoining room. On entering I found there, provided by the loving thoughtfulness of the Masonic brothers, assisted by their wives, every article that was needed for my mourning wardrobe. Such wholehearted chivalry, such knightly courtesy, seems indigenous to Southern soil and it blooms and flourishes there as it will some day the wide world over.

The Freemasons' Monthly Magazine, in honor of their esteemed brother, published the following:

At Wilmington, N. C., on the 27th [of] June last, [died] Major George W. Glover, formerly of Concord, N. H. . . . He was devotedly attached to Masonry, faithful as a member and officer of the Lodge and Chapter, and beloved by his Brothers and Companions. . . . Shortly after his decease, his lone widow returned to New Hampshire, and wrote . . . "never, never, shall I forget while reason lasts, the kindness of the Brethren at Wilmington."

It is interesting to note that although much of Major Glover's property was vested in slaves, his young widow refused to have anything to do with their sale. Years later Mrs. Eddy wrote, "I declined to sell them at his decease in 1844, for I could never believe that a human being was my property."[1]

Quietly the young widow returned to her beloved New Hampshire, and in the midst of the dark clouds found one bright ray of sunlight—the anticipation of a child, who was born three months after his father's passing. But when her baby arrived the young mother's joy did not long abide. For soon, through no fault of her own, they were parted.

With tears in her eyes, Mrs. Eddy many, many years later, related the circumstances leading up to her sepa-

[1] Message to The Mother Church for 1902, p. 15.

Earliest known picture of Mary Baker Eddy
taken about 1844

ration from her little son. As she herself was far too ill to give a mother's attention to her child, Mahala Sanborn, her nurse, was asked to care for him in her own home. As the condition of the young mother improved, she felt that she could undertake the task herself, and her boy was restored to her. By this time, however, the child, somewhat spoiled by Mahala's overindulgence, had become sufficiently boisterous and exacting to overtax the strength of his young mother, not yet recovered from the severe illness and nervous strain. There were additional circumstances which led to the final step by which Mary Glover was deprived of her child, the most important factor of all being the passing of the one she held most dear of all earthly friends, her mother.

One year after this new sorrow entered Mary Glover's life, her father, Mark Baker, married again and her old home took on a new atmosphere, friendly enough, but changed irretrievably. No longer was her little son welcome in her father's home. In view of this new situation, it was thought best that Mary should make her home with her sister Abigail, who had married Alexander H. Tilton, owner of the cloth mills at Sanbornton Bridge.

The Tiltons had a son of their own who was in rather delicate health, and this prompted Abigail to refuse to take her sister's romping and robust child into her household. And although this unsisterly decision seemed harsh to Mary Glover, she was helpless in the matter. She neither had the means to provide for herself and her son, nor was she strong enough to make her own way in the world. After a night of agony and prayer, the despairing mother kissed her baby boy farewell. Upon the insistence of her sister Abigail and with the advice of her father, Mark Baker, reluctantly she placed him once more in the care of Mahala Sanborn. Mahala, newly married, moved to a town about forty miles away in the mountains and took the boy with her.

The tragic separation from her little son, Mrs. Eddy later described in "Retrospection and Introspection" (pp. 20–21):

> The night before my child was taken from me, I knelt by his side throughout the dark hours, hoping for a vision of relief from this trial. . . . A plot was consummated for keeping us apart. The family to whose care he was committed very soon removed to what was then regarded as the Far West.
>
> After his removal a letter was read to my little son, informing him that his mother was dead and buried. Without my knowledge a guardian was appointed him, and I was then informed that my son was lost. Every means within my power was employed to find him, but without success. We never met again until he had reached the age of thirty-four, had a wife and two children, and by a strange providence had learned that his mother still lived, and came to see me in Massachusetts.

In the periods when her health would permit, the young widow endeavored so far as possible to contribute toward her own support. At one time she established what would now be termed a kindergarten class, the first school of its kind in New Hampshire. This is my recollection of what she told me about the school:

> It attracted much attention. At one time my sister's husband, Alexander Tilton, in passing came to the window and looked in. He saw forty little heads bowed in prayer with foreheads resting on their little hands, repeating "Our Father which art in heaven."

He went home and told my sister Abby what he had seen. Never after that was he heard to jibe at religion. The mothers of the little ones told me that when the children came home from school, they would take their Bibles and go into a room by themselves to read and pray. I had seen that the way to have children stop doing wrong is to have them love to do right.

The loss of a devoted husband, the passing of her mother, and the enforced separation from her only child were indeed tragic experiences for Mary Glover. Although she did not know it, these afflictions were but the first drops in the cup of earthly sorrow she was destined to drink.

Under these circumstances Mary Glover's stay with her sister was not a very happy period in her life. Abigail Tilton was a kind enough sister just so long as Mary humbly conformed to the rules of the household and did not venture to express too freely an opinion of her own. But after the freedom and happiness of her own home, Mary's position in Abigail's house was far from ideal, particularly when she thought of the cruel separation from her child that her sister had demanded. No wonder that her health did not improve under these conditions. Destiny, however, had another sad experience in store for Mary Glover.

About this time she met Dr. Daniel Patterson, a relative of her father's second wife, who was a dental surgeon of some repute and a man of keen intellect. He finally induced the young widow to marry him when he assured Mary's family that her ill-health was caused by brooding over her child and that, once they were married, he would provide a home for the little fellow. This seemed such convincing proof of Dr. Patterson's generous character that Mary Glover married him, but her fondest hopes for reunion with her son were never realized. Dr. Patterson failed to keep his word, pretending that his wife's health was too delicate to permit her to care for the boy.

Once more established in a home of her own, Mary Baker (now Mrs. Patterson) began to play an active part in the abolition movement. Her feeling against slavery and her sincere conviction that it must be uprooted, once more impelled her, in spite of the conservatism of her father and the disapproval of Abigail Tilton, to employ her writing talents in exposing the evils and dangers of the system. Feeling was becoming intensified both in the North and in the South, as the years of the Civil War approached. When the dangerous fissure, which had been widening during the strife-torn years of the late fifties, finally severed the last thread of unity, and the newly formed Southern Confederacy ordered an attack upon Fort Sumter, the Civil War with all its horrors began to tear at the heart of the nation.

Early in 1862, Dr. Patterson was commissioned by the governor of New Hampshire to distribute a fund for "loyalists" in the Southern States. While on this mission he was taken prisoner, and it was months before he managed to make his way back North again. One evening Mrs. Eddy gave us a graphic description of that trying experience, which in substance was as follows:

My husband, Dr. Patterson, had received an important commission from Governor Berry to visit the South and reimburse the Southern men who had been true to the Union and had suffered

When she lived with her sister Abigail Tilton
about the year 1853

the loss of their property and their slaves. Arriving in Washington, he and two friends decided upon a visit to the Bull Run battle-field. While they were viewing the historic spot, my husband saw cavalry in the distance and notified his companions, who laughed at his fears. However, as the horsemen approached them rapidly they sought to escape, but were brought to a halt with bullets. This flying cavalry scouting company took my husband's gold watch, ripped open the waistband containing the money Governor Berry had given him, took every dollar, and marched him away to Libby prison, from which he was later transferred to Salisbury prison.

One dark night he and two companions made their escape. In a short time the companions gave up the struggle to escape; but my husband, urged by an indomitable will, braved danger, suffered hunger almost to starvation, endured cold and disease, but at last walked to the Union lines in Pennsylvania. He weighed before the capture two hundred and six pounds and came home weighing but little more than half his former weight. So changed by his suffering was he that his brothers did not know him. His escape was called one of the most remarkable of the Civil War. The news of my husband's capture came to me when I lay sick in bed.

Lying on an invalid's bed, she could do little to aid her husband; but she wrote to her relatives, asking them to do something in his behalf. In spite of the many blunders and unfulfilled promises of Dr. Patterson, she expressed for him a wifely devotion and affectionate concern. Her loyalty and bravery in saving his life on one occasion were recorded in some of the New England papers under the heading "Female Bravery":

A North Groton [N. H.] correspondent of the Concord Patriot writes that on the 20th ult., Dr. Patterson, a dentist in that place, while employed in splitting wood before his door, was assaulted by two men, father and son. . . . The elder . . . rushed upon him with a shovel, which the Doctor knocked from his hands with his axe, at the same time losing hold of the axe. . . . [The son] rushed upon the Doctor with the axe, and striking him upon the head, stunned and felled him to the ground. The father then seized him . . . and called upon his son to strike. The son was about to comply . . . when the wife of Dr. Patterson, almost helpless by long disease, rushed from her bed to the rescue of her husband, and throwing herself before their intended victim, seized, with unwonted strength, the son who held the axe and prevented him from dealing the intended blow. Help soon came, the assailants fled, and the feeble but brave wife was carried back to her bed.

But in spite of her loyalty and patient forgiveness of her husband's failings, there came a time when the weakness of his nature led him into an immoral situation which could not be overlooked. Mrs. Eddy once told me the story of Dr. Patterson's infidelity which was submitted as evidence when she was granted a divorce. This is my recollection of her account:

One morning on leaving home, Dr. Patterson said, "You need not expect me back tonight. I have some business and I may be gone for several days." That day he eloped with one of his patients. The husband of the woman, that night returning home, missed his wife, and taking an officer, started in pursuit, found them, and brought his wife back home.

A few days later, a lady called at my home whom I did not at first recognize. She was pale and very haggard. "Do you not know me?" she asked. I replied that I did not. Then she told me her name.

"Why have you come to me, you who have robbed me of my husband and desolated my home? You who have disgraced yourself and your family."

She replied, "I have come to you because of what your husband has told me of you. I know you must be a good woman and I felt you would help me." I asked her what I could do for her. She said, "My husband has locked me in my room and only gives me bread and water each day. Today, with the help of the servants, I escaped to come to you and ask you to go to my husband and ask him to forgive me."

I told her that I would do all that I could for her. The following day I went to her husband's factory, for he was a wealthy man and a member of one of the leading families of Lynn. I did not find him in and was told that he had gone on business to Boston. Later he called at my house and said, "I came to ask you if you have really forgiven your husband and can you forgive my wife her cruelty to you?"

"I forgive them both," I replied, "and I ask you to forgive them." He left me and my heart went out to him. I went to God in prayer for that husband and his home. Soon after, I heard that his wife had resumed her place in his household, for the cruelly wronged husband had forgiven her and their home was again a happy one.

And so ended another preparatory period of Mary Baker's life, a long stretch of dreary years, during a large share of which she suffered both physically and mentally.

In the midst of her years of invalidism, she had always pondered deeply and prayerfully the meaning of God's will and had humbly searched and striven to understand the working of Providence. But her search, up to the year 1866, had not been successful. Only occasional glimpses of light came to her seeking thought during those lonely years.

But fortunately for the welfare of mankind, the outlook (as so frequently happened in this wonderful woman's life) was always at its blackest just before the dawn.

CHAPTER III

THE year 1866 marks a turning point in human history, the beginning of an era of incalculable significance to the welfare of mankind, for in that year an event took place in the life of Mary Baker Eddy of more importance to the world than any other occurrence since the advent of Jesus Christ.

For some time before 1866, in her vain search for health, Mrs. Eddy (then Mrs. Patterson) had paid several visits to a magnetic healer named Phineas P. Quimby of whom she had heard some remarkable stories. Encouraged by Mr. Quimby to expect a healing, Mrs. Eddy did at first obtain temporary help, but she soon suffered a relapse, and later realized that whatever benefit she received was due more to her own faith in God than in Mr. Quimby's forceful assurances and head manipulations. As a matter of fact, the basis of Mrs. Eddy's lifelong researches had been along spiritual lines and while willing to concede only the highest motives to Mr. Quimby, she came to understand how essentially foreign to his doctrine were the things that she held sacred. After a temporary sense of confusion, the Quimby mist vanished and although always appreciative of his good intentions, Mrs. Eddy at length fully perceived the gulf between teachings based on the human mind sense of government and spiritual understanding based on the one Mind's omnipotence.

Up to this point Mrs. Eddy's whole life had been one consistent, progressive preparation for the supreme moment when the light of Christ, Truth, dawned on her consciousness. And her unceasing yearning for a clearer sense of God was destined to be realized when on February 1, 1866, in Lynn, Massachusetts, she met with a severe accident which threatened to end fatally. On her way to a meeting of the Good Templars (a temperance organization) she slipped, fell on an icy pavement, and was picked up unconscious. *The Lynn Reporter* of February 3, 1866, published the following account of the now historic incident:

Mrs. Mary Patterson of Swampscott fell upon the ice near the corner of Market and Oxford streets on Thursday evening and was severely injured. She was taken up in an insensible condition and carried into the residence of S. M. Bubier, Esq., near by, where she was kindly cared for during the night. Dr. Cushing, who was called, found her injuries to be internal and of a severe nature, inducing spasms and intense suffering. She was removed to her home in Swampscott yesterday afternoon, though in a very critical condition.

In spite of all that the doctor and kind friends could do, her dangerous condition continued until her life was despaired of. On the Sunday after the accident Mrs. Patterson asked to be left alone with her Bible. Turning to the second verse of the ninth chapter of Matthew she read the account of the healing by Jesus of the man sick of the palsy. In that sacred moment a divine revelation flashed upon her receptive consciousness, broke the thrall of disease and suffering, and produced an instantaneous healing.

The persistent study of her Bible was the open door

through which poured in this revelation of the truth of being, which Mrs. Eddy afterward named Christian Science. Never did she claim, however, that that wonderful instant of revelation marked the fullness or completion of her discovery. On the contrary, her discovery of Christian Science was the result of Bible study, revelation, and growth. It was not a case of instantaneous conversion in which she could say, "Now the past is nothing,—begin entirely anew." She demonstrated each step of the way.

During twenty years prior to her discovery Mrs. Eddy had, as she explained later, "been trying to trace all physical effects to a mental cause."[1] She had experimented with many forms of hygiene and materia medica only to find them all wanting. One day, many, many years after her healing, she opened the copy of her textbook and read to her household the following passage:

> He learned that suffering and disease were the self-imposed beliefs of mortals, and not the facts of being; that God never decreed disease,—never ordained a law that fasting should be a means of health. Hence semi-starvation is not acceptable to wisdom, and it is equally far from Science, in which being is sustained by God, Mind.[2]

This account was not unlike Mrs. Eddy's own experience. For many years before her discovery she lived according to hygiene and for a time ate nothing but bread. When she found Christian Science she was an absolute slave to physiology and hygiene. In matters of diet and exercise she followed all the rules. After her

[1] "Retrospection and Introspection," p. 24. [2] Science and Health, p. 221.

discovery she decided that following these rules was not Science, but what should she do? Friends urged her not to drop them all at once, to stop by degrees. But she saw that "Science is Science,"[1] and so dropped forever physiology and hygiene. "After this," she said, "I wish you could know the work I was able to do, working night and day for the Cause."

It was shortly after her fall and healing that Dr. Patterson finally deserted her. They had come to a definite parting of the ways. The instability of his character made it inevitable, but it was not until 1873 that Mrs. Patterson was granted a divorce. At that time the court gave her the right to resume her former name of Glover.

Gathering together the freshly broken strands of her life after Dr. Patterson's desertion, and girding herself for the task which, instinctively, she knew awaited her, although as yet she could not define it, Mary Baker Glover now took lodging in the house of Mr. and Mrs. George D. Clark of Summer Street, Lynn, Massachusetts.

She knew that the revelation of the truth of being that had dawned on her had to be apprehended practically, and in terms so understandable that its illumination might reach all mankind. *How* was the healing done, and *how* could it be repeated? With unswerving devotion she sought the answers to these questions in humble prayer to God.

Seated at the large table in the Clark home, among other boarders, was a man named Hiram S. Crafts, destined to become the first pupil of the Discoverer and

[1] Message to The Mother Church for 1901, p. 22.

Founder of Christian Science. Though a simple worker in a shoe factory in Lynn, of ordinary intelligence and common school education, Hiram Crafts was an apt and receptive student, eager to learn all he could about God. It was in order to help him that Mrs. Glover began to write down notes on passages in the Scriptures, giving their spiritual meaning as it was unfolded to her. Not only did she reveal to him these spiritual interpretations, but she also instructed him how to heal the sick, and for a considerable time, under Mary Glover's guidance and encouragement, Hiram Crafts practiced healing successfully.

Even after the divine revelation that came to Mrs. Eddy in 1866, the writing of her textbook, "Science and Health," did not proceed in the facile manner of an ordinary literary achievement. No, indeed! It was a herculean undertaking. When it is realized that Mary Glover had no precedents to guide her, no nicely documented works to refer to, and no living human being with whom to discuss her problems, the magnitude of this noble woman's task instantly becomes apparent. Through her own persistent, prayerful study of the Bible she had to discover the *modus operandi* of spiritual healing and prove it every step of the way before she could set it down in such a manner that it could be understood and demonstrated by others. This, indeed, was not the work of a moment. It was the consecrated labor of years; years of unending effort and constant study, of poverty and privation, of scorn and ridicule, of misunderstanding, suspicion, desertion, and betrayal.

In her long search before she discovered the Science of Mind-healing, she investigated materia medica, scholastic theology, spiritualism, and mesmerism, in fact, she tested almost every phase of material belief which the human mind presents. And finding them untenable, one by one, she rejected them all. The tortuous course Mary Glover had to pursue before she made her great discovery was a long and trying one.

Mesmerism was one of the human systems she was compelled to look into. In view of her experiences, and the numerous critical references to mesmerism and hypnotism found in her writings, it seems incredible that even the most skeptical scoffer at Christian Science could ever have accused Mrs. Eddy of employing mesmerism in her healing work. Even in her childhood she refused to have anything to do with mesmerism, and the following story, as I afterward recorded it, is ample proof of the fact:

When I was a mere child, my father, hoping to help me, sent for the mesmerist who had brought this fatal doctrine into New Hampshire. It was known that he had performed such deeds that he was looked upon as a magician. At first, I refused to have anything to do with him, but on my father's earnest petition I submitted. For three weeks he undertook to mesmerize me, but entirely without success. He would come at night and make passes over me and say, "If I could only get her to sleep." He could in no way affect me and gave it up without accomplishing anything.

From friends and acquaintances, during those years of labor and research after she had experienced her remarkable recovery, came no word of encouragement, sympathy, or comfort. If there were one or two willing to listen to Mary Glover's teaching, there were many more who ridiculed or scoffed. Added to other trying experiences were indignities heaped upon her by students for whom she made many sacrifices. While she was visiting in Worcester, Massachusetts, she related many years afterward to the members of her household that a disaffected student went to the superintendent of the insane asylum and represented to him that she was insane, and engaged him to call upon her to investigate her sanity with the purpose of placing her in confinement. Although he was announced as an ordinary visitor might have been, his first step was to take hold of her wrist and feel her pulse. As she commenced to talk with him upon his method of caring for the insane, however, he became deeply interested in her talk and soon confessed to her the conspiracy, telling her on leaving that he was greatly indebted to her for much help from which he should profit.

During all those years when the world doubted, ignored, or condemned, Mary Baker Glover remained faithful to the vision God had entrusted to her care. When one person refused to listen to her explanation, she patiently turned to another. Not the least of the hardships she had to overcome were the misunderstandings and false accusations of those with whom she lived. Indignity seemed to follow indignity. During one year, while she was writing "Science and Health," she was forced to move eight times.

In response to an earnest request, she went to live with Mrs. Sally Wentworth in Stoughton, Massachusetts, remaining for some two years. Even here Mrs. Wentworth's son, Horace, sneered at the guest and ridiculed his mother's interest in her doctrines, while a cousin, Kate Porter, who occasionally assisted Mrs. Glover in copying for her, frequently made fun of her behind her back. Mrs. Wentworth's daughter, Lucy, however, was a devoted friend and championed Mrs. Glover's cause in the home. Many years afterward, when attacked by pulpit and press, Mrs. Eddy commissioned me to visit these people, to secure from them the actual facts regarding her stay in their home, and to put these facts in writing. The following is the statement prepared in compliance with Mrs. Eddy's request:

To whom it may concern: On July 9, 1903, I saw Mrs. Horace Wentworth in her home in Stoughton, Massachusetts. In reply to my inquiries concerning the Reverend Mary Baker G. Eddy, she said, "Mrs. Eddy was certainly a wonderful woman, she stayed much by herself and spent most of her time reading the Bible and explaining it in a way which I did not understand and this was why I did not like her." Mrs. Wentworth also declared that Mrs. Eddy was a very neat person and always kept her room in good order. That I might have Mrs. Wentworth's statement as to Mrs. Eddy's conduct, I asked, "Did you ever know of Mrs. Eddy doing any damage to anything or harming anybody?" Mrs. Wentworth replied, "No, she never damaged anything nor did any harm to anybody that I know of."

In those early days the handful of followers who believed in Mrs. Eddy's teaching had no standing whatever in the eyes of the world. They were not known as a religious body; they did not even have a name, but were known simply as students of "Moral Science." When finally their teacher designated them as "Christian Scientists," they were looked upon as sacrilegious and Mrs. Eddy herself as a dangerous woman.

The little group of students had no public meeting place; they simply gathered in the front parlor of one or another of the homes of the members. Although the words of the "woman of Lynn" often made the hearts of her listeners burn within them, to others they were merely words, idle words, strange words, which they did not understand. The thoughts she voiced were new. Public consciousness was not then accustomed to grapple with metaphysics, although it was groping feebly in that direction. Those who did pause to listen frequently grasped her meaning only in such infinitesimal measure and so imperfectly that the seeds of Truth were either swallowed up by the cares of the world, choked by the thorns of materiality, or blown away by the winds of indifference. A few, studying in her early classes, although apparently discerning her meaning at first, later betrayed gross ignorance of the spiritual import of the teachings which she had so lovingly labored to impart to them. To some of these early students, this new system meant simply a means of regaining their own health, and afterward an opportunity to commercialize the knowledge they had acquired. The new teaching did not have a textbook to dignify and support it; it could be had only by word of mouth or through the study of a handwritten manuscript.

The actual writing of "Science and Health" began in February, 1872, and it was in the printer's hands by September, 1874; however, another year elapsed before the book came out. The publishers to whom she first applied said they could not understand it and would not attempt to publish it. Mrs. Eddy was very sorrowful and her pupils very indignant. At length, a sum was subscribed by Mrs. Eddy and some of the students, and a printer was found who consented to undertake this task.

When, in the fall of 1875, the "little book" finally appeared, a great step in the gigantic task of promulgating her teachings was accomplished. The little band sighed happily, but the tremendous task of making known to the world the teachings of Christian Science was only just begun. The book met with some favorable reviews, but was greeted for the most part with a storm of adverse criticism.

A notable exception was A. Bronson Alcott, whose warm sympathy and appreciation went out to Mrs. Eddy in this hour; she has told us of his visit and his greeting, "I have come to comfort you."[1] He had spoken of her, of her discovery and of her followers, in the library of Ralph Waldo Emerson at one of his Sunday evening gatherings. Mr. Emerson had heard of her book, "Science and Health," and the other members of the group listened to Mr. Alcott's remarks without criticism or small-minded prejudice. This led a little later on to an invitation from Mr. Emerson to Mr. and Mrs. Eddy[2] to visit him, which they were grateful to accept from the "Sage of Concord."

[1] "Pulpit and Press," p. 5.

[2] Several years after her divorce from Dr. Patterson, Mrs. Eddy thought it wise to accept the faithful love and unwavering devotion of her student, Asa G. Eddy, who offered to help her bear her ever-increasing burdens. The marriage proved to be a happy and wise step and Mr. Eddy continued to be all that he appeared, an honest, kind, strong, loyal companion during the five years of their married life until he passed away in 1882.

Whether people condemned or praised "Science and Health," Mrs. Eddy's estimate of the book never faltered. On one occasion, according to my recollection, she said to me:

I could not originate such a book as Science and Health. I have to study it myself in order to understand it. When I came to the writing of it each day, I did not know what I should write until my pen was taken up and I was ready to begin. It was divine Mind expressing itself.

When her textbook was first published, the very name "Science and Health" aroused such scorn and ridicule on the one hand, and such bitter resentment and animosity on the other, that the book had almost literally to pass through fire and flood, as it went on its healing mission to mankind. In her endeavor to overcome the prejudice in the public thought and to introduce the book to a doubting world, Mrs. Eddy directed her early students to go about from house to house offering it for sale wherever it might be received.

Long years afterward, Mrs. Eddy admonished a student never to forget to be grateful for the privilege of talking Christian Science to someone. Then she went on to say that when she was in Lynn in the early days, she wanted so much to talk to someone who would listen on the subject of Christian Science. She heard of one who lived five miles away. She walked there to find the woman so bitter against Christian Science that she shut the door in her face, so she walked the five miles back. Later on, at a happy gathering of the secretaries in her study in Concord, Mrs. Eddy said, as I recall:

One moment of eternity means untold good for millions. I remember that when I first started this Cause I used to say, "How happy I shall be if I can get only one interested in it." And I said, "Is not God interested in this, Mary?" And the answer came to me, "God is interested, and because of it your Cause cannot fail." This was always of great comfort to me. In those days some people would say to me, "Are you going insane?" as they spoke of my writing and teaching. But little by little the tide began to turn, and at last I could see that the Cause was established on a firm foundation and I was comforted.

Although at times in those early days her path was hedged about with the direst difficulties, the hand of wisdom was constantly guiding her footsteps. Although some of her early pupils disgraced her, turned away from her teachings, and temporarily held back the progress of her Cause, nevertheless her devotion to her students was untiring.

In the storm of misunderstanding and criticism, in the stress of ingratitude and betrayal; constantly tried as by fire; at times, all but overwhelmed by the waters of malice, envy, and hate; beset by poverty, homelessness, and loneliness, this woman pressed on. Healing cases her students had failed to heal, pondering and communing with her heavenly Father, she meekly broke the bread of Truth with her fellow men. In the face of opposition greater than the world had known since the advent of Christianity, she would not be swayed from her God-appointed task. In the secret recesses of her heart Mary Baker Eddy guarded the truth that God had revealed to her.

CHAPTER IV

Healers needed "**U**NLESS we have *better healers,* and more of this work than any other, is done, our Cause will not 'stand and having done all stand.' *Demonstration* is the whole of Christian Science, nothing else proves it, nothing else will save it and continue it with us. God has said this—and Christ Jesus has proved it."[1]

These significant words are quoted from a letter written by Mrs. Eddy, who was so thoroughly aware of the importance of demonstrating the truth God had revealed to her. Indeed, so revolutionary were her teachings that, had she not been able to offer proof of their truth, they would have seemed completely unconvincing. From the very first she began to test her discovery by healing others. As early as 1867, her first manuscript on Mind-healing, "The Science of Man," was in friendly circulation, although she did not take steps to copyright it until 1870. Even then she felt that the time was not yet ripe for its publication. "It was so new," she writes, "the basis it laid down for physical and moral health was so hopelessly original, and men were so unfamiliar with the subject—that I did not venture upon its publication until later, having learned that the merits of Christian Science must be proven before a work on this subject could be profitably published."[2]

[1] *The Christian Science Journal,* June, 1936.
[2] "Retrospection and Introspection," p. 35.

Soon after her own healing, therefore, Mrs. Eddy began to heal others. Living in the light of Spirit, she radiated that healing light; she could not do otherwise. The sick and the dying found a path to her door and went on their way healed and renewed in body and spirit. In "The First Church of Christ, Scientist, and Miscellany" (p. 105), she has written:

After my discovery of Christian Science, I healed consumption in its last stages, a case which the M. D.'s, by verdict of the stethoscope and the schools, declared incurable because the lungs were mostly consumed. I healed malignant diphtheria and carious bones that could be dented by the finger, saving the limbs when the surgeon's instruments were lying on the table ready for their amputation. I have healed at one visit a cancer that had eaten the flesh of the neck and exposed the jugular vein so that it stood out like a cord. I have physically restored sight to the blind, hearing to the deaf, speech to the dumb, and have made the lame walk.

In the pages which follow are recorded some cases of healing by Mrs. Eddy, a few of which have never before been published. Some of the cures I heard from the lips of those who were healed; others were testified to by close relatives of patients; still others were told to members of the household by Mrs. Eddy herself. To some of these cases of healing I was myself an eyewitness.

During those early days in Lynn, so numerous were Mrs. Eddy's beneficent works that, as she later remarked, "That city once resounded with my cures." One of these early healings she related substantially as follows:

When living in Lynn, the four and a half year old boy of one of my students was taken seriously ill with what was called brain fever. He had been a little tyrant. The mother cared for the child without avail, and at length came running to my home with the baby in her arms.

When she came in, she placed him on the bed saying, "I am afraid I have come too late. I think he is gone." And to all appearances the sick child had ceased to live. I told her to leave me and not to return for an hour.

After her departure I went to God in fervent prayer and very soon the boy sat up in bed. I told him to jump down and come to me. He came and I took him in my arms and was silently declaring that he was not sick, when I saw the little fellow double up his fist and strike at me saying, "I *is* tick, I *is* tick." Although he struggled and fought in my arms, love prevailed, and he was soon at play with some spools that I had made into a cart with a darning needle. I still continued treating him and again he came to me and struck me with his fist, saying, "I *is* tick, I *is* tick." Then I said, "You are not sick and you are a good boy." Then he fell at my feet limp and lifeless, and I took him in my arms and my thought went out to my heavenly Father. The boy soon returned to consciousness and was ready to play again.

When I saw his mother coming, I told him to go to the door to meet her. When she opened the door and found her child healed, she was so overcome that she nearly swooned and I had for a time another patient. On the way home her little boy talked of God and said how good God is.

In 1899, when Mrs. Eddy asked me to prepare an article on Christian Science and its Discoverer for publication in the "Concord Old Home Week Supplement" of the *Boston Traveler,* she gave me the following account of one of her early healings. As it finally appeared in the *Boston Traveler* it read:

About the year 1870, Mrs. Eddy was called to attend Mr. John Scott of East Stoughton, Mass., who was suffering from enteritis and stoppage of the bowels. When Mrs. Eddy was called, two doctors of medicine had just left his room, saying that he must die. For nearly two weeks there had been no action of the bowels, though the physicians had administered three doses of croton oil to accomplish the desired result. Mrs. Eddy found him vomiting, rolling on the floor, and at times shrieking in agony. He was using violent language, and almost cursing God. Mrs. Eddy asked him to cease, and said, "If you will be calm, I can heal you." Mr. Scott did as requested. In less than one hour the pain was entirely gone, the vomiting stopped, and the bowels acted normally.

Before Mrs. Eddy left . . . he declared that he felt perfectly well. The next day he attended to his business, and was out working on his farm. She gave the sufferer but one treatment, when he was completely restored. Remarkable as was the man's physical healing, even more remarkable was the transformation in his thought and life. His wife told Mrs. Eddy a few days later that she had never before seen him fondle his children as other fathers did, but on the night of his recovery he called them to him, and taking them in his arms, he told them that he loved them; and with tears rolling down his cheeks he said to his wife, "I am going to be a better man." It is not strange that the happy wife said to Mrs. Eddy, "Oh, how I thank you for restoring my husband to health, but more than all, I am grateful for what you have done for him morally and spiritually." For this service of love she refused remuneration, as was her rule. But she holds that this is no reason why others should not charge for their services, for Jesus hath said, ". . . the labourer is worthy of his hire."

About the year 1868, as Mrs. Eddy sat alone, quietly occupied in an outside room opening on a porch and a garden, the door was suddenly burst open, and an escaped maniac dashed into the room. For a moment he met her quiet, fearless gaze with a wild glare, then he fiercely seized a chair to hurl at her head. She spoke to him compassionately and he dropped the chair, approached her, and pointing upward, exclaimed, "Are you from there?" The next moment he was kneeling before this earnestly praying woman with his head pressed hard into his hands.

Very soon the poor fellow looked up into her face with the astonishment of sanity, and declared, "That terrible weight has gone off the top of my head." When he left her he was in his right mind. Later this man made a special visit to Mrs. Eddy to thank her for his healing.

Out on the highway, in front of Mrs. Eddy's home, a good many years ago, a teamster was one day run over by a heavily laden wagon from which he had fallen, the wheels passing across his body. The man was thought dead and the body was brought into her home and laid on the floor. Mrs. Eddy, who was upstairs at the time, was sent for. Looking away from the body, she began to declare the truth, and experienced such a wonderful sense of mental uplift that she became entirely oblivious of her surroundings. After spending some moments in this spiritual contemplation of Truth, she suddenly discovered that the man had arisen. Passing his hand over his eyes in a somewhat dazed way, he said, "Why, I thought I was hurt, but I am all right."

In the early days of her healing work Mrs. Eddy sought a clearer understanding of the *modus operandi,* that she might teach it to others. She said of this early experience that when she started to heal by argument her perplexity began. Before this, her silent, earnest, uplifted heart to God wrought instantaneous healing, and a sweet peace was hers. Then she came to see that mortal mind resulted in phases of matter, and the question of overcoming these phases presented itself. The answer was through understanding prayer to the divine Mind. Such prayer establishes man's oneness with his Maker. This is God's way, who knows nothing of matter. Her perplexity vanished and she saw clearly the significance of the admonition, "Flee as a bird to your mountain."

She went on to say that the little bird does not hop his way to the mountain; he flies straight and swift as an arrow. So in our healing, if the patient is reached through divine Love, the discordant condition "will vanish into its native nothingness like dew before the morning sunshine."[1] Jesus said to the man possessed, "Come out of him, and enter no more into him."[2] God "spake, and it was done; he commanded, and it stood fast."[3] This is true healing without relapse or reversal and it stands fast.

The very presence of this God-inspired woman healed the sick, not because of human personality, but because of the truth which she spiritually perceived. As the rays of the sun melt the snow and ice and warm whatever they touch, so did the purity of her consciousness bless and heal.

Many were the healings of those in Concord whom she happened to see as she rode through the streets in her carriage, and upon whom her illumined thought momentarily rested. The crippled, the insane, the helpless invalid "whom Satan hath bound," all were freed by the love which this woman radiated. Upon rich and poor, enemy and friend alike, it shone. A milliner, whom I knew, who told me of her healing, had been confined to her room with consumption. She was sitting all wrapped up at the window one day with her last will and testament in her lap, thinking of nothing but her approaching

[1] Science and Health, p. 365.　[2] Mark 9:25.　[3] Psalms 33:9.

end. At this time Mrs. Eddy's carriage drove into the street. As it passed, Mrs. Eddy looked at this woman and her sympathy and love went out to her. The invalid thought, "What is it this woman has that I have not?" At once the thought came to her, "I will try Christian Science." Then, although it was winter and the snow was on the ground, she went to the closet and put on her coat, rubbers, and hat. Although she had not been out of doors all winter, she hurriedly went to the Christian Science Reading Room, where she asked questions about Christian Science. At this time she was so uplifted that she returned home and prepared her husband's dinner. When he came in, he thought his wife was out of her mind, and it took her a few days to convince him that all was well. I am happy to be able to testify that she was indeed thoroughly healed.

There was a woman in Concord who had an appointment to meet me at Christian Science Hall. Her illness was such that it was very difficult for her to walk up the four or five steps leading into the building. When she arrived, I was standing outside the hall and informed her that Mrs. Eddy was about to pass in her carriage and it would be the patient's privilege to see her as she rode by. In a moment or two the carriage approached, and as Mrs. Eddy passed by she smiled at the woman and greeted her. As the carriage disappeared in the distance I stepped over to the patient and said, "Now we will go into the hall and you may have your treatment." The patient replied, "I don't need a treatment. I am well." At which I smilingly remarked, "This is the way I lose my patients."

On a certain occasion Mrs. Eddy, accompanied by a student, went to a furniture shop to select some chairs, where they were waited on by a man who was wearing a bandage over one eye. As they were being shown the chairs, Mrs. Eddy seemed so absorbed that she paid little attention to them, replying to a question as to which she liked best with the words, "Any that we can sit on." Later when the student reproached Mrs. Eddy with her lack of attention to the business in hand, she replied, "Could I think of chairs when the man was suffering?" When the student returned the next day to order the chairs, the salesman asked: "Who was that lady with you yesterday? I had an abscess on my eye and when she went out, I took the bandage off, and there was not a sign of it left."

From time to time it was the privilege of the members of Mrs. Eddy's household to hear from her own lips accounts of her healing work. She frequently took opportunity to speak of these experiences at the dinner or supper table, when the household were gathered together, or when alone with a single student in her study. Many of these experiences date back to the earliest days of her ministry of helpfulness. On one occasion she said, as I recall:

I was called sometime in the fifties to attend a child who was a great sufferer from bloodshot and inflamed eyes. I used no medicines whatever, but in response to my prayer to God the young child was completely healed. For this healing I would accept no pay, but the mother, out of deep gratitude, presented me with a beautifully embroidered petticoat.

Years later Mrs. Eddy, in speaking of her healings, pointed out many times that the first error held by a patient is the false belief that man created him and that life is here in the form of mortality. Instead, she taught that we have to know that this material birth, existence, and death are all an illusion and the opposite of Truth. In time we shall see that this illusion has nothing to do with man, but is the opposite of man. This false concept should be destroyed, so that man and the Principle of man can be understood.

On one occasion, Mrs. Eddy related to me the following case of healing which I afterward wrote down:

In the absence of Dr. Quimby from Portland, a man was brought to the hotel where I was staying, who was in a pitiable condition. He had sometime previous met with an accident and he was well-nigh broken to pieces. His knees and ankles were out of place and he was suffering untold agonies. The proprietor of the hotel came to me and besought me to do something for the poor sufferer. At first I thought I could not. Then I said, "God can do it." I went to his bedside and lifted my thought silently to God. At the conclusion of my prayer I said, "Now you can arise and open the door for me." The man arose, and with the iron clamps he wore rattling as he walked, went and opened the door.

Mrs. Eddy's healing of a woman of dumbness in Lynn, about the year 1867, was related to me many years later by her son. She had been treated by many physicians without relief, when a friend proposed that she see Mrs. Eddy. People seldom turned to Christian Science in those days until all other hope was exhausted, for Mrs. Eddy was considered a strange woman. So desperate was his mother's condition, however, that she asked for treatment from one of Mrs. Eddy's students. The student found difficulty in handling the case. Each day when the woman, who was then a girl, returned from a visit to the practitioner, the first words of her mother were, "Fannie, can you speak?" Fannie would sadly shake her head in the negative. At last it was decided to call on Mrs. Eddy for help.

On the day of her return from her visit to Mrs. Eddy, the daughter was again greeted with the old question, "Fannie, can you speak?" Instantly the answer came back, "Yes, I can," and she continued, "When Mrs. Eddy saw after my treatment that I still could not speak, she suddenly said with authority, 'In the name of God, speak!' Instantly I spoke my first word, saying 'Oh!'" After that experience the patient found herself fully healed.

It was as natural for Mrs. Eddy to heal as for most people to see and speak. Receptive to God's guidance, ears open to His message, she was ever seeking to be more and more obedient, to love more, to understand God better. As one studies Mrs. Eddy's words and gains some slight apprehension of her spiritual nature, one is better able to understand how this woman's state of consciousness accomplished two such healings as I made note of soon after she had related them to me. The first healing as I recorded it was as follows:

I was called by a brokenhearted mother to attend her young son who was afflicted with ankylosed joints. The bones of the knees appeared to be solidified and the verdict of the doctors was, "a hopeless case—the boy will never be able to walk again." I treated the little fellow and told his mother that she need have no further fear, for her son would be able to walk and run with other children. Three days after, the boy was playing in the yard with his companions. An acquaintance who saw him romping with his friends asked him what business he had to be out there and told him to go into the house, and stay there. The response from the little fellow was: "You are not my doctor. Mrs. Eddy is my doctor, and I can play if I want to." Sometime later his mother brought him to me to thank me for his wonderful healing. As he walked across the floor, I noticed that he toed in with one foot, and spoke to him of it. He said: "My mamma said I should tell you about that. I have always walked that way." I told him to walk in the right way, just like the other boys. He did so at once, being healed instantaneously, and ever after walked naturally.

This is my account of the second healing:

I was visiting in the house of a dear friend, a Quaker lady who was so afflicted with hip disease that she could not go up and down stairs except with the greatest difficulty and then only by going up sideways slowly, step by step. After talking with her of God I said to her, "Now you can walk upstairs as other people do." She replied: "Mary, I have always believed thee, but now I cannot believe thee. I can never walk as others do." I told her that she could go upstairs if she only would. At last she said, "I do believe thee now and I will try." Not without amazement to herself and to her friends, she went upstairs in the natural way and came running down again. Her healing was instantaneous and permanent.

When Lord and Lady Dunmore of London, England, visited America with their two young daughters, they went to Concord, New Hampshire, to call upon Mrs. Eddy. She told them of certain cases of healing which she had brought about. Among these was that of a child whom she restored to life and health after it had passed on. When Mrs. Eddy was living in Boston on Columbus Avenue, she was much interested in a little child in the neighborhood whom she had often seen in a baby carriage and whom she had learned to love dearly. As she missed the child and her mother for several days, she called at the home to inquire after their welfare. But the mother met her at the door in great sorrow, saying that her little one had died and the doctor had just left. When Mrs. Eddy said she would like to see the child, the mother replied that it was too late—nothing could be done for her. But as Mrs. Eddy persisted in her request, the neighbor reluctantly admitted her to the room where the dead child lay.

Requesting the mother to leave her alone with the child, Mrs. Eddy took the lifeless little body in her arms while her thought went out in earnest communion with divine Love. Lost in prayer, oblivious of material surroundings, but wholly absorbed in the consciousness of infinite Truth, Life, and Love, Mrs. Eddy was recalled to earth when the child sat upright in her lap saying, "I want to see my mother." Mrs. Eddy summoned the mother and placed the child on the floor saying, "Now run to your mother," which the child did with perfect freedom. When in London in the spring of 1929, my wife and I visited Lady Dunmore and reminded her of this incident. She then told us that there was something more of interest in that wonderful case of healing, for when the child ran to its mother she said that it was the first time the child had ever walked.

Mary Baker Eddy's motto as a Christian Science practitioner was *semper paratus*. She did not have to prepare herself to heal. She was already prepared. A striking instance was seen in her healing of Mr. Calvin A. Frye soon after she moved to Chestnut Hill. He was found by a member of the household on the night of November 9, 1908, unconscious and apparently in a death stupor. Three of us strove to restore him, but he seemed to have passed on.

When Mrs. Eddy was notified, she arose and was about to dress, but decided there was not time to do so. She asked that he be brought to her, whereupon Calvin was lifted into a small rocker and drawn into the chamber to which Mrs. Eddy had retired for the night. Mrs. Eddy, then in her eighty-eighth year, commanded Mr. Frye, with the voice of authority, to rouse himself, to awaken from his false dream. At first she met with no response, but this did not discourage her. She redoubled her efforts and fairly shouted to him her command that he awake. In a few moments he gave evidence of life, partly opened his eyes, and slightly moved his head. Seeking to rouse him, Mrs. Eddy said, "Calvin, don't commit self-murder." He replied, "I don't want to live."

"Disappoint your enemies and live," she commanded. "Say that you do want to stay and help me."

Then he took his first stand and answered, "Yes, I will stay." It was now about a half-hour since Mr. Frye had first been found. Mrs. Eddy told him to work for himself, and Calvin uttered the words, "Yes, I will come back." Soon he walked back to his room unaided. He retired, slept through the night, and arose the next morning in time to be down for breakfast at seven o'clock. After breakfast he was busy going over his accounts, and when I asked him to cash a check, he readily did so, thus showing his complete return to normality.

It is most inspiring to recall that throughout the entire experience Mrs. Eddy manifested tremendous spiritual strength and poise. Those of us who were present on that occasion can testify that this remarkable woman had lost none of her healing power in her eighty-eighth year. She spoke in strong, clear tones. There was no fear, no doubt, no discouragement; only absolute confidence, only perfect assurance of the victory of Truth. The following morning Mrs. Eddy was up at the usual hour, and at nine o'clock, when I entered her study, I found her busily occupied in reading her Bible. She called my attention to verses 7 and 8 of Psalm 138, which she marked in pencil:

> Though I walk in the midst of trouble, thou wilt revive me: thou shalt stretch forth thine hand against the wrath of mine enemies, and thy right hand shall save me. The Lord will perfect that which concerneth me: thy mercy, O Lord, endureth for ever: forsake not the works of thine own hands.

Quite as remarkable as the case of Calvin Frye was the instantaneous healing by Mrs. Eddy at Chestnut Hill of another member of the household before our very eyes. One morning when we were all called into the study, one of the workers seemed indisposed. She had all the appearance of suffering from nervous prostration or great exhaustion. Mrs. Eddy saw the sufferer's condition and called her to her side. Then she spoke to her with decision, rebuking the error and calling her to come out from the mesmerism and to be her true self.

While we stood there, a change gradually came over the patient. Mrs. Eddy continued to rebuke the error, called to her in terms of love, until she was completely healed. What most impressed those of us who were present was the extreme simplicity of Mrs. Eddy's healing work. So clear was her understanding of the divine Principle of healing, that it often needed but a single statement of truth to bring about the desired results.

In the year 1897, Mrs. Eddy invited her followers to visit her at Pleasant View on Independence Day. That year the Fourth of July came on Sunday and Monday was observed as the holiday. I well remember the occasion. Among those who took the journey was a mother, accompanied by her two children.

When they were about to start from their home in the Middle West, it was discovered that the small daughter, seven years old, had a very sore spot which protruded from the head and was very much inflamed. All the way to Concord she would not allow her curly head to be combed, crying bitterly whenever the attempt was made. Although the mother tried to meet the condition through prayerful mental work, yet in the morning, when they were to go out to Pleasant View, the swelling had enlarged until it stood out from her head and was more inflamed than ever. As the mother felt that the hair must be combed that morning, she took the scissors and cut the hair away around the sore spot and then washed and combed the hair as gently as possible. The whole thing was a most trying ordeal and it was only through showers of tears that the little one was finally made ready to go. A light straw hat, with a wreath of daisies on it, could not be worn because it hurt her head.

After the speaking was over at Pleasant View, Mrs. Eddy sat upon the porch and greeted the people as they passed through the porte-cochere. The mother was preceded in the line by her children. When these two little ones, a boy of nine and the girl of seven, arrived in front of Mrs. Eddy, they stopped the whole procession and stood looking up into her face smiling joyously. Mrs. Eddy looked at them and then looked at the mother, and smiled back at the children, as someone told them to pass along. This is the mother's account of her illuminating experience:

I wish I could make the world know what I saw when Mrs. Eddy looked at those children. It was a revelation to me. I saw for the first time the real Mother-Love, and I knew that I did not have it. I had a strange, agonized sense of being absolutely cut off from the children. It is impossible to put into words what the uncovering of my own lack of real Mother-Love meant to me.

As I turned in the procession and walked toward the line of trees in the front of the yard, there was a bird sitting on the limb of a tree, and I saw the same love, poured out on that bird that I had seen flow from Mrs. Eddy to my children. I looked down at the grass and the flowers and there was the same Love resting on them. It is difficult for me to put into words what I saw. This Love was everywhere, like the light, but it was divine, not mere human affection.

I looked at the people milling around on the lawn and I saw it poured out on them. I thought of the various discords in this field, and I saw, for the first time, the absolute unreality of everything but this infinite Love. It was not only everywhere present, like the light, but it was an intelligent presence that spoke to me, and I found myself weeping as I walked back and forth under the trees and saying out loud, "Why did I never know you before? Why have I not known you always?"

I don't know how long it was until my boy came to me and said, "Come, mother, they are going home." I got into the carriage and drove back to the hotel, but that same conscious intelligence and Love were everywhere. It rested upon everything my thought rested on.

When we got back to the hotel, there was no boil on my child's head. It was just as flat as the back of her hand. . . . For weeks it had a strange effect on me. I could not bear to hear anyone speak in a cross, ill-tempered tone, or do anything that would cause pain. . . .

Each time I saw Mrs. Eddy I had a wonderful revelation of God. I know she was no ordinary woman. God had anointed her with the oil of gladness above her fellows, for she "loved righteousness, and hated iniquity." [1]

A healing which I recall with much interest occurred in the year 1907, at the time of the "Next Friends Suit," when many newspapers were sending their reporters to Concord in the hope of securing interviews with Mrs. Eddy. Since it would have taken nearly all her time if she had seen all these representatives of the press, she appointed me as a receiver and giver of messages. At this time there were three or four reporters particularly determined to see Mrs. Eddy. They had been sent to Concord to "dig up" the truth about her. The orders from the city desk were positive; they were, "Use whatever methods are necessary, but get the facts!" If Mrs. Eddy was dead and someone was impersonating her, if

[1] Hebrews 1:9.

she was mentally incompetent and physically in ill-health, they were to bring back the story, sparing no one.

As one of these men remarked later: "We hoped that something of a sensational nature would be uncovered. If Mrs. Eddy was merely living in a saintly retirement, working and praying for mankind, it was not news. But if any of the other rumors about her were true, it would be a great story." This man said they were a belligerent lot of old-timers, and they hoped and expected to "dig up" a lot of scandal; that they were news hounds baying on the trail.

Having been in Concord for some time, covering the occurrences surrounding the suit, and trying to get whatever information they could about Mrs. Eddy, this reporter said they were all greatly amazed at the kind and loving treatment accorded them. "If ever anyone has a right to hate someone, surely the Christian Scientists had a right to hate us," he said. "We were there to vilify Mrs. Eddy if we could. We had no reverence and no decency. We did not believe anything but the worst about anybody, and we wanted if possible to hold Mrs. Eddy up to scorn and ridicule, to expose and denounce her."

The chief man among this group, representing a big New York newspaper, was known as a particularly hard-boiled reporter and a steady drinker. He had been afflicted for some years with a cancerous growth of the throat, which was extremely painful and at times overwhelmed him completely.

One evening as they were all sitting in his room at the Eagle Hotel, drinking and smoking, bored with their stay, this man was suffering with his throat; he had lost his voice entirely and was unable to speak a word. Mrs. Eddy had asked me to call these men by telephone and inform them that it was impossible for her to see them. But she cautioned me at the same time, "Be sure to ask for the leading man and speak directly to him."

The telephone rang and one of the younger reporters answered the call. According to instructions, I asked to speak to the head man, whose name he mentioned, but was told that this man was too ill to come, could not come, and could not speak if he did come to the telephone, and could not speak any way. Remembering Mrs. Eddy's instruction I said, "Tell him to come to the telephone; he can hear what I say even if he can't talk."

Accordingly, the suffering newspaper man came to the telephone, showing decided anger (as I was later informed). He listened for a few moments. Those in the room, of course, could not hear what was being said, but when this man turned away from the telephone, he not only could speak perfectly, but was healed.

The healing stirred these men. They sat around, looking at each other, unable to comprehend what had happened and more startled by it than anything else. They had of course heard that Christian Scientists claim to heal the sick, and they knew that their comrade had been healed.

One can imagine the consternation and excitement produced by this sudden transformation of one of their number. These men had believed Mrs. Eddy to be only a humbug, and the reputed healings of Christian Science to be a great hoax. Their whole position was overthrown by this proof offered before their very eyes. They packed their bags and left.

Some years later a relative of this man called at my office in Boston, and gave me the following message: "My uncle requested me to see you and to tell you that in his last days he turned to Christian Science, and he knew that he owed a debt of gratitude to Mrs. Eddy for his healing in Concord."

We may perhaps most fittingly close this recital of some of Mrs. Eddy's healings by quoting her words from one of her letters:

> May the light of Divine love so illumine your mind that you behold yourself in His likeness, even as you are,—the image of perfect Mind. Thus will you find all power, wisdom, and peace in goodness, and demonstrate the grace of Spirit as ever sufficient to help you in every time of need.[1]

[1] *Christian Science Sentinel,* July 25, 1936.

CHAPTER V

FROM the moment of her discovery of the great truth of spiritual being, Mrs. Eddy's one overwhelming longing was to share it with others. And to those who were willing to receive it, she imparted the truth as naturally as the sun gives out light and heat.

Mrs. Eddy was what is known as a "born" teacher. She once told me that even when a young girl, she loved to help others gain an understanding of the Scriptures. This gift for teaching was beautifully illustrated in the case of the young chore boy employed by her father. The little fellow could not read or write and knew nothing of the Scriptures. Mary Baker taught him by reading aloud to him chapter after chapter from the Bible. The boy was so inspired by this loving instruction and took such an eager interest in his lessons that before long he was able to read and write. From then on, every Sunday found him in his place in the old meeting house. Mary Baker's hours of loving labor given to this lad bore ample fruit, for he afterward became a successful lawyer. And some years later when Mary Baker suddenly found herself a widow among strangers, one of the first messages of sympathy she received was from the former chore boy at her old Bow home.

When Mrs. Eddy first began to teach her early students to heal disease by spiritual means, the method of practice for these students perplexed her. She herself performed the healing work with ease and rapidity through her own exalted thought and spiritual intuition, but her students could not be taught up to the silent effectual prayer that casts out evils and heals the sick, till their hearts and minds were prepared for it. And since these students did not possess these spiritual qualities, she knew that she must bring about a spiritualization of thought to equip them to do the healing work.

This was the task which faced Mary Baker Eddy, the task which God had assigned to her. She saw that a *modus operandi* as well as inspiration is essential to accomplishment, until one reaches that exalted state of consciousness whereby one is able to heal through the realization of the truth, with absolute clarity and certainty. And so she set herself to the task of working out practically by precept and example the rules and method for the application of this Principle to the ills, sins, and tragedies of mankind. Mrs. Eddy's arduous labors along this line finally resulted in the writing of "Science and Health." Thus she has made available to every seeker the rules that enable him to overcome these evils through the power of God.

Among her early students were some who were too material to grasp the truth presented, and they rebelled against the teaching. Others, saturated with scholastic theology, wasted the hours in argument and hair-splitting. But those who were ready, drank in the truth as flowers absorb the dew. One of Mrs. Eddy's early students, a keen businessman, once said to me that the days spent in her classroom were the best of his whole life, that while there he felt as if he were living in a world where only good was present. He said that it seemed to him that he could never again do a mean or unjust thing.

Although Mrs. Eddy did not teach during the two and a half years while she was engaged in the actual writing of her textbook, she began teaching immediately afterward and kept on doing so for a period of fifteen years. Over the door of the little house on Broad Street, Lynn, which she purchased shortly after the manuscript of "Science and Health" was placed in the printer's hands, she erected a sign which read, "Mary B. Glover's Christian Scientists' Home." Here, during the spring of 1875, she taught a class. Six more years she remained in Lynn, teaching, supervising the work of students, healing cases too difficult for others, organizing the little band into a church, revising "Science and Health," and laying the foundations of the great work of promulgating her teachings. It was at 8 Broad Street, in January, 1881, that she established her Metaphysical College under the seal of the Commonwealth.

By 1882, her work had outgrown the bounds of Lynn (the little group had prior to this expanded beyond the parlors of its members to a public hall in Boston) and Mr. and Mrs. Eddy moved to Boston, which henceforth became the headquarters of the Christian Science movement.

On Columbus Avenue, Boston, then a pleasant residential street, she reopened her College. For nearly nine years she bore the entire burden of the College, teaching many students who came from all parts of the United

When she was preaching in Boston, 1882

States, attracted by the healings performed by earlier students, some of whom she sent out into fields distant from New England. In addition to teaching, she lectured Thursday evening in the parlors of the College and preached on Sunday whenever she could find the time. During these years she was also revising her textbook, writing other works, establishing *The Christian Science Journal,* editing and writing articles for it. In 1889, after due deliberation, she closed the doors of the Massachusetts Metaphysical College, then at the height of its popularity.

During these years Mrs. Eddy taught a number of clergymen who had become interested in her teachings. She was always happy to have ministers of the Gospel as her students. Nor as a rule would she accept any tuition fee from them for instruction in the Massachusetts Metaphysical College; and if two persons made application, with one of them a minister, and only one could be admitted, the clergyman was usually the one favored.

There were, however, some clergymen during those years who were bitterly denouncing Christian Science and its Discoverer. Led by three ministers who were determined to drive Mrs. Eddy from Boston, they organized an attack upon her which continued over a period of months. They charged that Christian Science was only a fad; that it was founded upon the personality of Mrs. Eddy and that when she was gone it would disappear into oblivion; that she was a pantheist; that she was prayerless and that she did not believe in the atonement. It is an interesting fact that these attacks helped the Cause of Christian Science, and earned for Mrs. Eddy the kindly support of clergymen of the same faith as those who so bitterly attacked her.

The clergy's condemnation of her work and her disappointment in some of those whom she had taught made no difference in Mrs. Eddy's attitude. She did not lose her desire to help them. When they turned to Christian Science, she welcomed them. At her request several were among the First Members of The Mother Church, two were appointed to the Bible Lesson Committee, one was placed on the Board of Trustees of The Christian Science Publishing Society, and two were elected to the office of President of The Mother Church.

As additional proof of Mrs. Eddy's friendly attitude toward the clergy, she once told me a story, which was substantially as follows:

While I was stopping in Washington, D. C., with my husband, Asa G. Eddy, we attended the church formerly frequented by President Garfield. The clergyman was introduced to us and begged the privilege of paying us a call, which request was gladly granted. He early took the opportunity of visiting us and spent the afternoon in listening to our explanation of the Bible and Christian Science. He asked the privilege of remaining to the six o'clock dinner, explaining that he enjoyed the sociability of the occasion though he could not partake of the repast, saying that for years he had been troubled with a stomach difficulty which the physicians declared had developed into cancer of the stomach. He avoided all hearty food and confined himself exclusively to a fluid diet.

All this he told us just as we were preparing to go to the dining room. I said to him briefly that this was an excellent opportunity to put to a test our talk of the afternoon. He replied by saying that he hardly could consent to test the doctrine for the sake of killing himself. However, I voiced the truth and asserted his ability to eat in comfort. He went with us to the table, soon forgot himself and his false fears and partook heartily of the salad, meat, and pastry. At the conclusion of the dinner he said, "What have I done? Will I ever survive?" We assured him there was no danger. He felt no harm and never was again troubled.

Mrs. Eddy was always lovingly eager to share with the members of her household the result of any new illumination of the Scriptures which had been revealed to her. Often the entire household would be called in; sometimes it would be just one member who, she felt, especially needed the explanation, rebuke, or loving encouragement which she had to impart.

Turning to the Bible in time of need, she taught the members of her household to do likewise. "Search the Scriptures," she would say, "for they testify of divine Science. They are my sole teacher, in learning even a little of its infinite Principle."

One beautiful winter's morning, I was invited into the study. The sun was streaming in through the tower windows. Mrs. Eddy was seated in her chair with an open Bible in her lap. She greeted me with a radiant smile, and her first words were those of praise for the beauty of the morning. Then she said, as I later made careful note:

I was thinking this morning of some who are not where they should be. And my dear Book of books opened at the twenty-fourth chapter of Matthew.

Taking up her Bible Mrs. Eddy read:

Blessed is that servant, whom his lord when he cometh shall find so doing.

Verily I say unto you, That he shall make him ruler over all his goods.

She went on to say that whenever Jesus spoke in commendation to students, he also pointed out the consequences of failure. He says:

But and if that evil servant shall say in his heart, My lord delayeth his coming;

And shall begin to smite his fellowservants, and to eat and drink with the drunken;

The lord of that servant shall come in a day when he looketh not for him, and in an hour that he is not aware of,

And shall cut him asunder, and appoint him his portion with the hypocrites: there shall be weeping and gnashing of teeth.[1]

She continued by saying it was her work not only to encourage right doing, but to rebuke error. Those who accept, go higher; those who are full of resentment and justify self, fall by the way. She spoke not only of the beauty of holiness, the beauty of goodness, and her joy in abiding in that dear Presence, but also of the necessity to descend into the valley and heal the demoniacs.

I was prompted to remark, "The drunken are those who are overcome of self and sin," and she replied that they most certainly are, for had not the prophet spoken of those "drunken, but not with wine," meaning those who are intoxicated with evil desires and thoughts? It is of these who live in the senses that it is written, "nor drunkards, . . . shall inherit the kingdom of God." Those who live in the senses cannot enter into the kingdom of Truth. Therefore, seek to arouse the stupefied one, and he who awakens is saved. The Scriptures are the authority for this, since it is written in the twelfth chapter of Hebrews (6–8):

[1] Matthew 24:48–51.

For whom the Lord loveth he chasteneth, and scourgeth every son whom he receiveth.

If ye endure chastening, God dealeth with you as with sons; for what son is he whom the father chasteneth not?

But if ye be without chastisement, whereof all are partakers, then are ye bastards, and not sons.

She continued her exposition by saying that those who do not endure chastisement are not sons, for they are not the legitimate offspring of Truth, as their works testify. Those who endure chastening shall live in the spirit, not in the senses.

On another occasion Mrs. Eddy asked me, "What is disease?" I replied that disease was not genuine; it was but a counterfeit. She said: "Yes, disease is but the image of a lie. It is not matter or a part of matter. It is but the result of a falsehood. As Jesus said, it is but 'a liar and the father of lies.' There is no truth in it. Disease, sickness, and sin are to be recognized as the image of wrong thought, and seeing it thus, it is destroyed."

One December morning, after weeks of exacting labor for the Cause, Mrs. Eddy called the household into her study. The open Bible lay in her lap and her sweet face was aglow with joy and peace. She said she had called us to her so that she could explain the passage from God's word on which her eye first rested that morning. She said each day before she began her work she turned to her Bible for direction and guidance. Then she would open the textbook and see the wonderful manner in which they harmonized with one another. This particular morning her Bible opened to the fourth chapter of John, verses 35 and 36:

Say not ye, There are yet four months, and then cometh harvest? behold, I say unto you, Lift up your eyes, and look on the fields; for they are white already to harvest.

And he that reapeth receiveth wages, and gathereth fruit unto life eternal: that both he that soweth and he that reapeth may rejoice together.

She read these verses with considerable feeling and at the conclusion said in substance as I later recorded:

Behold, how clearly the heavenly Father has spoken to me this morning in these words, "Say not ye, There are yet four months, and then cometh harvest? behold, I say unto you, Lift up your eyes, and look on the fields; for they are white already to harvest." Observe that our harvest is already here if we will but see it. It is but our blindness that delays the reaping. See this, and "Look on the fields; for they are white already to harvest."

If you have a case that seems protracted, lift up your eyes and realize the eternal presence of peace and harmony. Know that the harvest time of health and life is even now with you. Then "he that reapeth receiveth wages, and gathereth fruit unto life eternal." The fruit you gather is not for the moment, it is for eternity. And furthermore, these blessings are ours now, "that both he that soweth and he that reapeth may rejoice together."

One time she told us not to say there is too much or too little of anything. She said: God governs. He knows best. He will do all things right.

When upon one occasion a student showed signs of resentment after receiving a merited rebuke, I recall that Mrs. Eddy said:

When a student rebels at the teacher who has carried the Cause for forty years, who is right, the student or the teacher? Learn this lesson, that it is error which brings the sense of resentment and to resist resentment is to take sides with God. But when the teacher points out an error, and the pupil disputes it, then the error is increased.

[74]

Human will is error, nothing. To manifest human will is to go against the teaching of Christian Science. To resist human will is obedience to this teaching.

Speaking of loyalty to the Cause of Christian Science she often voiced in substance to the members of her household thoughts similar to this:

Loyal students speak with delight of their pupilage, and of what it has done for them, and for others through them. By loyalty in students I mean this,—allegiance to God, subordination of the human to the divine, steadfast justice, and strict adherence to divine Truth and Love.[1]

The following verses from John 7:24–26 so inspired Mrs. Eddy one morning that she called in all the members of the household to expound them to us:

Judge not according to the appearance, but judge righteous judgment.

Then said some of them of Jerusalem, Is not this he, whom they seek to kill?

But, lo, he speaketh boldly, and they say nothing unto him. Do the rulers know indeed that this is the very Christ?

Her comments as I remember them were:

The very Christ is the true idea of God. This idea is ever as much present as is God. Light always has its reflection. Where there is no reflection, then there is no light. When one does not express the reflection then he is not expressing love.

Then she questioned us all, "What do you lack most, faith, hope, or love?" We answered, "Love." "Yes," said Mrs. Eddy, "having the understanding of love, you establish health and peace." "What was it," Mrs. Eddy continued, "that made Jesus the Messiah?" The answer given was, "His spiritual

[1] "Retrospection and Introspection," p. 50.

understanding." "I will give you the answer," she replied, "the true answer in the language of the Bible: he 'loved righteousness and hated iniquity.' " Then she proceeded to explain that the true Christian not only loves the right, but that he hates iniquity and is willing to uncover the evil in himself and in others. She made it clear that he was not a true disciple who closed his eyes to wrong-doing and took no steps to unmask the wrong-doer and bring to an end the evil-doing. She further commented that in Christian Science we are not to draw back from our duty of exposing error and thus causing it to be destroyed, from fear of adding fuel to error's flames, whether it appears likely to harm us or the Cause of Truth. We are to do right and leave the consequences to God. Referring to the necessary rebuke of error, she said, as I later wrote down my impression of her words:

> One of the hardest things I have had to do was to deal with this very question. I would rather at any time dwell on love alone and get away from error, but that would not do; it would allow error to increase. Jesus rebuked sharply; I must do so until I arrive at that place in Mind where I cannot see error, where God, Spirit, is All-in-all. The omnipresence of good involves the nothingness of evil, but the mental argument must be used until you can heal instantaneously without it.

In this connection, she spoke of the Christian Science work at one of the jails and of the interest which the prisoners took in the Sunday services regularly held there. She said that she would have more hope for one of those prisoners than for a jealous, self-satisfied Christian. Indeed, she had more hope for a pagan, for one who has never heard of Christ, than for one who knowing the divine law yet persisted in breaking it.

Mrs. Eddy was at all times practical in meeting the human need. One morning, in referring to a restful night which she had experienced, she spoke somewhat as follows:

sleep and dreams

> I had a restful sleep all last night and it is right to sleep restfully and soundly. Is there any difference between the night dream and the day dream? When we awake from a night dream, we see its unreality; the day dream of pain and disease is no more real. Science is here to show us the way of attaining the image of God, not through suffering, as did Jesus, but through spiritual understanding.

On one occasion, repeating a verse from the ninety-first Psalm, she made clear to us the spiritual import of the verse which ends with the words, "shall abide under the shadow of the Almighty." She said the truth is that we "shall *abide*," for in eternal Truth there is no shadow. We shall abide in Truth, for we have but one consciousness; we realize we are united to divine Love, then we shall have health perpetual, no lapsing but abiding harmony.

Discussing, at another time, some of the erroneous doctrines prevailing in human systems of thought, she read from II Timothy 4:14, 15:

work not with matter Spirit important

> Alexander the coppersmith did me much evil: the Lord reward him according to his works:
>
> Of whom be thou ware also; for he hath greatly withstood our words.

and then commented in substance:

[77]

Alexander, the matter worker. Let us not work in matter. Which is the more real, matter or Spirit? Now watch that you give the pre-eminence to Spirit. Weight must be placed on the side of Spirit.

Often when members of her household were gathered together, Mrs. Eddy would question us as to our methods of healing. These questions brought out many illuminating statements from her and instruction of inestimable value, which were eagerly seized upon by those who listened to her. On one occasion, Mrs. Eddy said, as I afterward noted:

There is one infinite Life and that Life is eternal and that Life is my Life.

When visiting a patient who is very low, never say, "There is no death." Realize, "All is Life and Life is eternal." To say, "There is no death," is to call up the image patients fear. And their fear may produce the effect they dread. Just as we see that which is reflected on the retina of the eye, so the thought given a patient is reflected by him.

Calling the members of her household together one New Year's morning, Mrs. Eddy opened her Bible to Solomon's Song 8:12–14, and read:

My vineyard, which is mine, is before me: thou, O Solomon, must have a thousand, and those that keep the fruit thereof two hundred.

Thou that dwellest in the gardens, the companions hearken to thy voice: cause me to hear it.

Make haste, my beloved, and be thou like to a roe or to a young hart upon the mountains of spices.

And then I recall she commented:

Material existence is a dream and unreal, while the spiritual fact of Life is eternal. This spiritual fact is not attained by death, but by a conscious union with God, who is Life, Truth, and Love.

[78]

Now is the day to attain this realization. Now is the time to prove our faith by our works. "Now is the accepted time;" therefore now is the moment to improve every opportunity.

Again opening her Bible, this time to Proverbs 2:11, 12, she read:

Discretion shall preserve thee, understanding shall keep thee:
To deliver thee from the way of the evil man, from the man that speaketh froward things;

and turning to page 227:14–19 of Science and Health she quoted:

Discerning the rights of man, we cannot fail to foresee the doom of all oppression. Slavery is not the legitimate state of man. God made man free. Paul said, "I was free born." All men should be free. "Where the Spirit of the Lord is, there is liberty."

"What a beautiful passage for the New Year," she commented, as I afterward recorded. "What new step are you to take for the New Year?" A member of the household replied, "A step higher in spirituality." "Yes, a step out of sense," she approved, "a step into actions, not words. When I was a girl, I would sometimes hear someone sing and sing a song over until I wearied of it. So I weary of words without deeds. Can you think right and do wrong? Can you think wrong and do right? No. Once a little boy in school was whipped for whistling. Said he, 'I didn't whistle, it whistled itself.' So if you think wrong, the wrong will come out, but if you think right, the right will externalize itself."

One bright morning, I remember, we were all called into the study and found Mrs. Eddy particularly joyful. "First I want to hear some poetry from our *Monitor*,"[1]

[1] *The Christian Science Monitor.*

she said, after we had all assembled: and then she read a poem, without glasses, and with excellent expression. "How fine that the readers of the *Monitor* can have such bright verses," she commented. "I used to be called a good reader of the Scriptures. I had a fine instructor in reading, Mr. Sol Wilson. If there was in the reading any false tone, he would catch it and then *we* would catch it."

Turning now to the more serious business of the occasion, she said quietly that she wanted to say something from God to help us. She quoted the verse from Scripture which says: "I am the way, the truth, and the life: no man cometh unto the Father, but by me," and continued by saying that in our journey we seem to be climbing a hill, and there is but one way and that is straight up to the top. Now what attitude of mind should we have to make our demonstration? She answered her own question by saying that, above all, we must heed the First Commandment, "Thou shalt have no other gods before me." Then we must have obedience, and third, we must love. Finally, we should know that we are already at the top, then we shall not feel weariness in the climb.

At another time, Mrs. Eddy told us that whenever she had anything to do, if she thought there was any human will about it, she left it undone. On the other hand, if the work demanded a great sacrifice, this sacrifice did not hinder her from doing her duty.

To the members of her household, individually and as a group, Mrs. Eddy voiced many helpful words of timely rebuke and warning against the danger of lapsing into indifference and temptation through neglecting to obey Jesus' admonition, "Watch." She said in substance:

> You must examine yourself and learn what are your temptations and errors; then rest not until you take up arms against them. Put all under your feet that is not worthy to be called Truth, wisdom, and Love. Practice this when alone. Do not think it wearies you to practice the truth by which you heal the sick, and that to turn away from this to lightness and frivolity rests you. This is error and belief—not Science.
>
> "My yoke is easy, and my burden is light," were the words of him who taught and demonstrated the Science of God.
>
> Do not seek this Science for riches or emoluments, but as a means of doing good. Be willing to render up your all on the altar of Truth, for it is Science to know that what you sacrifice for this will be rewarded seven-fold; and that if you love money or the world's applause better than Truth, then you are not ready to come and follow Christ, the Way, the Truth, and Life.

At one time Mrs. Eddy addressed a long series of questions to each member of the household as to how he might do better than he was doing, seeking to emphasize to the workers that they must put into practice the truth they knew. She was much pleased with the answer which someone quoted from page 323 of Science and Health: "In order to apprehend more, we must put into practice what we already know."

One member of the household asked Mrs. Eddy whether a child should be instructed to say that he is God's perfect child, and she replied that we should always tell the spiritual facts of Science to the children. She said she had never known a child who did not understand Christian Science if given to him in the right way.

She once contrasted sympathy and compassion by referring to the feeding of the multitude by Jesus, by saying that Jesus had compassion and fed them; had he sympathized with them, he would have suffered because of their hunger.

In everything that she said and did, Mrs. Eddy was a shining example of common sense. Her profound understanding of spiritual things did not isolate her from the comprehension of her fellow men. Quite to the contrary; in conversation with her students, her language was always simple, and to the one who listened earnestly, easily understood. She protested against using involved terms and complex phraseology. I remember she once said that when she wrote for the public, she was compelled, through the necessities of the situation, to write absolute Science, and therefore she must use language and employ terms that were precise and exact in their scientific use and application, but when she was addressing an individual, she always adapted herself to his understanding and spoke so simply that he was sure to grasp her meaning. When we are talking to one who is not a Christian Scientist, in speaking of a disease, she continued, we are not to say that So-and-so has a belief. Say plainly that he is sick. And she quoted Paul's admonition, "I had rather speak five words with my understanding . . . than ten thousand words in an unknown tongue."

Again, her well-balanced, practical common sense was manifested when one of her students called upon her at her home on Commonwealth Avenue, Boston. The day was bitterly cold and the visitor felt uncomfortably aware

[82]

of that fact. She was overcome with chagrin that in calling upon the Founder of Christian Science she should in any way notice the cold, and felt she deserved a rebuke for giving heed to it. To make matters worse, when ushered into the parlor she found the room much lower in temperature than her own home. While her card was being taken to Mrs. Eddy, she thought, "I suppose Mrs. Eddy is so scientific, she does not know that it is cold. What will she think of me for shivering?" Soon Mrs. Eddy entered, warmly dressed in an eiderdown garment. Her greeting was, "Why, my dear, how cold this parlor is! The furnace must be started up at once. Let me give you this warm wrap. There, now I hope you are more comfortable!" Then, having provided for the human need, Mrs. Eddy gave undivided attention to her caller's mission.

[handwritten margin note: Mrs E. made guests comfortable + warm]

Mrs. Eddy was fearless in handling the claims of malicious arguments of evil and she taught her students to be equally fearless and wise. The health and harmony manifested in her home were outstanding.

[handwritten margin note: fearlessly handle malicious evil]

She taught the members of her household that when they properly kept watch over their thinking, they cleared their thought of the belief in evil and thereby let in the light of Truth. I recall that she said:

> The problem is not solved until the whole rule is demonstrated. You must overcome the arguments of evil and thus gain a balance on the side of God, good.

After one of the severe assaults made upon Mrs. Eddy, when a member of the household went to her with kindly sympathy, Mrs. Eddy replied somewhat as follows:

Every argument to hurt anyone [if reversed] does that one good. All things shall and do work together for good to them that love good, as the Bible teaches.

Sin and sickness are not infectious. We do not catch sickness or sin; good alone is catching.

Divine Love governs. This is the law of Christ and it is fulfilled and it cannot be reversed.

There is one Mind, in all, over all, and governing all.

Remember that malice exultant is no greater than malice defeated, both are false. But to know and understand that malice is nothing is to defeat it.

We can and do trust in our God to deliver us from the persecutions of those who war against Truth and Love.

The holy sense of God as All and Love, and that there is no other Mind, is the best way to meet the malicious arguments of evil.

When healing seemed slow and the burden heavy, she counseled her household substantially as follows:

The law of God says, "Bear ye one another's burdens, and so fulfil the law of Christ."

The law of evil whispers, "You cannot help Mrs. Eddy, neither can you help yourself." Now if you let this law of evil govern you and master you, you cannot fulfill the law of Christ; you cannot be a Christian Scientist.

Should the thought come to you that you cannot help yourself, then know that you have your reply in the Scripture, that even as Jesus said, "I can of mine own self do nothing," but "the Father that dwelleth in me, he doeth the works." Since God is omnipotence, there is no power or person that can hinder His healing work.

In a letter which Mrs. Eddy once wrote, she made it clear that there is only as much power to evil as we give it. She wrote:

Did you but know the sublimity of your hope; the infinite capacity of your being; the grandeur of your outlook, you would let error kill itself. _Error comes to you for life, and you give it all the life it has._

On another occasion she spoke of the great possibilities which lay before us in our work as Christian Scientists. She said we should be instruments of much good to the world. One student replied, "Yes, if we have love enough." She responded, "Love alone is not sufficient. You must also manifest divine wisdom if you would be of real service to others."

At a meeting of the National Christian Scientist Association held April 13, 1887, a question was asked Mrs. Eddy which "related to the prayer of Abraham, that if fifty, or even ten righteous men could be found in Sodom, that city should be saved from destruction."[1]

Mrs. Eddy's answer is of profound import to all nations and peoples. Her reply as reported in *The Christian Science Journal* was that "salvation was in proportion to moral weight," and she continued, "A life or a nation is saved, in proportion to the predominance within of purity, patriotism, or other right motives; and this is the inner spiritual meaning of the story of Abraham's petition to God. If Sodom City had in it enough moral worth, it would be saved, not otherwise."

It was a momentous occasion in November of 1898 when Mrs. Eddy sent the following to a selected group of her followers:

Beloved Student:

Can I see you in my room at Christian Science Hall, Concord, N. H., on Sunday afternoon, Nov. 20th at 4 p.m. Strictly confidential.

[1] *The Christian Science Journal* for May, 1887.

As soon as you receive this letter wire me yes or no. Business *most important*. Be free from engagements till after middle of that week.

The invitations contained no hint of what was in store and no explanation of our Leader's intention. I immediately wired, "Yes," and, notifying Mrs. Eddy that I had an engagement to lecture in Providence, Rhode Island, on November 22, asked if I should cancel it. The following telegram came in reply, "Make your present appointment there a little later. M. B. Eddy."

At the appointed hour the students, with no knowledge of Mrs. Eddy's purpose, had, with one accord, joyously answered her call. From far-away California, Texas, Georgia, and other states they came, as well as from Canada, Scotland, and England. Although the class included Christian Science teachers, practitioners, former clergymen and doctors, judges, editors, and lawyers, they seemed in scientific understanding on the level of untaught children, when compared with the wisdom and spiritual stature of their teacher.

The purpose of the gathering was not to teach the letter of Christian Science, Mrs. Eddy said, for the members were supposed to possess that knowledge. It was rather to spiritualize the Field, and she remarked to me afterward that her work with that class changed the character of the entire Field. The giving of this class was Mrs. Eddy's freewill offering to God. Although there was not one in the class who would not gladly have paid the fee of three hundred dollars for the privilege of instruction from Mrs. Eddy, and although there were thousands of others who would have considered the fee a small one for instruction from such a teacher, yet she declined, saying, "I do not want this class to be an affair of money at all."

The class, on assembling, listened with rapt attention to the following letter from Mrs. Eddy, which was read by Mr. Edward A. Kimball:

Beloved Christian Scientists:—

Your prompt presence in Concord at my unexplained call, witnesseth your fidelity to Christian Science and your spiritual unity with its Leader. Before informing you of my purpose in sending for you I waited for your arrival, in order to avoid the stir that it might occasion those who wish to share this opportunity, and to whom I would gladly give it at this time, if a larger class were advantageous to the students.

You were invited hither to receive from me one or more lessons on Christian Science, prior to conferring on any or all of you, who are ready for it, the degree of C. S. D., of the Massachusetts Metaphysical College. This opportunity is designed to impart a fresh impulse to our spiritual attainments, the great need whereof I daily discern. And I have waited for the right hour, and to be called of God to contribute my part towards this result.

The secret place, whereof David sang, is unquestionably man's spiritual state in God's own image and likeness, even the inner sanctuary of Divine Science, wherein mortals enter not without a struggle or sharp experience, and wherefore they put off the human for the Divine. Knowing this, our Master said: "Many are called but few are chosen." In the highest sense of a disciple, all loyal students of my books are indeed my students, and your wise, faithful teachers have come to so regard it.

What I have to say may not require more than one lesson, this, however, must depend on results; but the lessons will certainly not exceed three in number. No charges will be made for my services. Please be in the hall to-morrow at 1 p. m.

With love, Mother,

Mary Baker Eddy.[1]

[1] *The Christian Science Journal,* December, 1898.

The lessons were given in two sessions, the first lasting two hours and the second four hours. This class was the first Mrs. Eddy had taught since she closed the Massachusetts Metaphysical College in 1889. At the conclusion of the class, in awarding the degrees of C. S. B. and C. S. D., Mrs. Eddy bestowed the degree of C. S. D. on those who had previously studied with her, and who had fulfilled the necessary requirements. The degree of C. S. B. was conferred on the remainder of the class.

Promptly at four o'clock on Sunday afternoon Mrs. Eddy quietly entered the little hall, accompanied by two members of her household. Simply but tastefully gowned in dark material, she wore a bonnet of the prevailing mode. She had passed the threescore-and-ten milestone by more than seven years, but her step was light, her form erect, her brow serene, and her bright eyes flashed with intelligence and love. She was the picture of refinement and distinction; the embodiment of meekness and purity, completely devoid of human will power.

While the waiting company silently stood, Mrs. Eddy took her seat alone upon the platform. Smiling cordially, she motioned with her hand to the members of the class to be seated. She then requested each one to rise as his or her name was called, as there were some present whom she had never met. Then she began to teach.

Those who were privileged to sit in that class felt that not only a marvelous and inspiring interpretation of the Decalogue and the Sermon on the Mount had been put before them, but that the whole Bible had been held up in vivid review. No one could listen to Mrs. Eddy's teaching for very long without seeing how Christian Science absolutely coincides with the Holy Scriptures and agrees in every respect with the teachings of the Master. She went directly to the Bible for striking illustrations. She quoted Moses, David, Jesus, Paul, and John to elucidate her points, and revealed the inner meaning of well-known Scriptural passages. She put forth the Sermon on the Mount, the parables, the inspired word of John and Paul so convincingly that the listeners felt as though never before had they understood anything more than the letter of the Scriptures. At one point in her teaching, she called upon several members of the class to give the spiritual interpretation of a Scriptural passage. The students did exceedingly well, but when they had concluded Mrs. Eddy gave so luminous, so forceful, so practical an interpretation of the passage, that everyone present felt a distinct spiritual uplift.

Mrs. Eddy explained that in Christian Science we are learning to speak the language of Spirit, and told us that we must strive to express it as accurately, as spiritually, as possible. She spoke of the inadequacy of the literal translations of the Bible, and the great importance of gaining its spiritual meaning.

Presenting the seven synonyms of God, she asked each one of us, "What is God to you?" It was an inspiration to watch her face as different students answered. When replies were given clearly and understandingly, Mrs. Eddy's face glowed with joy. And after everyone had answered, she said as I recall:

Many wonderful things have been told me today. Now you must live up to them and prove them. That is what Christian Science is. It is practical. God is Life, and there is no evil.

Mrs. Eddy in her classroom never allowed an atmosphere of heaviness or dullness. As a teacher she was the embodiment of vivacity as well as of wisdom. Her method of teaching was her own, imparting the truth by questions and answers.

She endeavored to teach her students to let go of finite personality and let the impersonal Christ, Truth, speak. She told us not to think of her personally nor look to her personally for help. If we did, our thought would be darkened. She said we are all one in divine Principle, Love; one in demonstration. The light had come to her, but we must not look to her as the light. If we did, this would hinder our progress, even as turning away from her teachings would darken our thought.

The first day's teaching on the subject of Love she concluded somewhat as follows:

Love is the Father, who is strong in His care for His children and provides for every need. Love feeds, clothes, and shelters every one of His dear ones. Love is a Mother tenderly brooding over all Her children. This Mother guards each one from harm, nourishes, holds close to Herself, and carefully leads along the upward way. Love is a Shepherd who goes forth into the darkness of the night, into the storm and wind, to find the lost sheep. This Shepherd of Love leaves the beaten path, searches the wood and marsh, pushes aside the brambles, and seeks until the lost is found; then He places it within His bosom and returns to heal and restore.

"What is the best way to bring about an instantaneous healing?" she asked. There were many answers, but when

Thanksgiving Day, 1891

they had finished, she said that it is to love, to be love and to live love. There is nothing but Love. Love is the secret of all healing, the love which forgets self and dwells in the secret place, in the realm of the real. But it is not mere human love that heals, she pointed out, not a love for a person nor for anything—it is Love itself. The realization of this love for a moment will heal the sick or raise the dead.[1]

Here a member of the class asked, "Is there to be no discrimination made between good and evil?" She answered: "Ah, you have asked me that which is the hardest thing in Christian Science. Evil must be seen and denounced. The Bible says that Jesus was God's chosen 'because he loved righteousness,' but it also says he 'hated iniquity.' Wisdom as well as love is necessary."

As she continued to expound the meaning and teachings of Love, the members of the class discerned, more clearly than ever before, the meaning of all the scorn, envy, persecution, reviling, and hate that had been showered upon this woman who loved humanity well enough to endure all things for the sake of bringing healing.

This wonderful class closed with expressions of deep gratitude to their teacher, as the one through whom the healing power of Truth was revealed to this age. As she shook hands in farewell with each member, there was an expression of great joy on her beloved face.

[1] Miss Clara Barton, celebrated philanthropist and first president of the American Red Cross Society, although not a Christian Scientist, said of Mrs. Eddy in an interview appearing in the *New York American* of January 6, 1908: "Love permeates all the teachings of this great woman,— so great, I believe, that at this perspective we can scarcely realize how great."

CHAPTER VI

MRS. EDDY writes in her Message to The Mother Church for 1902 (p. 15): "Before entering upon my great life-work, my income from literary sources was ample, until, declining dictation as to what I should write, I became poor for Christ's sake."

It is a matter of record that long before her discovery of Christian Science and the publication of her epoch-making textbook, Science and Health, Mrs. Eddy was an accomplished writer. In an article which she wrote for the *Independent Statesman* in 1898, she says, "When I was a girl, Mr. Lane, editor of the *Belknap Gazette,* would ask me to write for his newspaper during political campaigns." Later on when the Hon. Isaac Hill, editor of the *New Hampshire Patriot,* asked her to contribute to his paper her "goose-quill would wag, however weely, for Pierce and King."[1] Her numerous contributions of poems, articles, comments on subjects of local or national interest, were solicited and published by the newspapers and magazines of her day.

In 1850, twenty-five years before her book, "Science and Health," was published, there was published in Manchester, New Hampshire, a book of poems and prose entitled "Gems for You," a collection comprising selec-

[1] Franklin Pierce, President of the United States, 1853–1857. William Rufus King, Vice President under President Pierce, who passed on soon after taking his oath of office.

tions from Horace Greeley, N. P. Rogers, James T. Fields, Hosea Ballou, Sarah J. Hale, and others, in which appeared two poems of which Mary Baker Eddy, then Mrs. Glover, was the author. The inclusion of Mrs. Eddy among prominent New England writers of that era indicates that she was an accepted author long before her discovery of Christian Science. Years later, I ran across a copy of this little volume, "Gems for You," and presented it to her. Having entirely lost track of these old poems of hers Mrs. Eddy was delighted with the little book and sent me a letter of appreciation.

In the volume of poems was one called the "Old Man of the Mountain," which Mrs. Eddy was inspired to write as she sat in the valley far below the well-known "Profile Rock," which stands high on a mountain at Franconia Notch, New Hampshire. The first verse reads:

> Gigantic sire, unfallen still thy crest!
> Primeval dweller where the wild winds rest,
> Beyond the ken of mortal e'er to tell
> What power sustains thee in thy rock-bound cell.

Her lines well recall the sculptured face boldly etched against the New Hampshire sky.

When, in the mid-nineteenth century, Mrs. Eddy discovered the great spiritual truth of being, her God-imposed task and whole endeavor from that moment were so to expound this truth that mankind might be blessed. In this sacred undertaking she encountered opposition. The carnal mind was stirred to the depths by this spiritual truth which challenged its very right to exist.

Very little help or encouragement came to her in those hours, and even a few of her early students urged her not to spend her time upon a book which few would ever read, and nobody ever understand. They told her not to waste her precious moments when she could so much better employ her energy in other ways. Even those who knew and loved this woman failed her; every obstacle which human ingenuity could devise was thrown across her path to obstruct her progress. But divine inspiration continuously pouring in impelled her to press on.

Years after this experience, when the world had begun to glimpse, through lives recalled from the grave, redeemed from sin, and reclaimed from despair, the divine nature of the truth she taught, Mrs. Eddy, recalling the days of poverty, hardship, persecution, and ridicule, wrote, "There is scarcely an indignity which I have not endured for the cause of Christ, Truth."[1]

In recognition of Mary Baker Eddy's achievements in the field of writing, she was at one time appointed an honorary member of the New England Woman's Press Association. Those familiar with her writings know that they exhibit a unique literary style. *Harper's Weekly*, a publication of national repute, in a tribute to Mrs. Eddy's utterances dealing with the death of President McKinley, said:

All the preachers preached on President McKinley; all the editors wrote about him. There was a great deal to say, and most of it seems to have been said. Of course thousands of writers and speakers said about the same things, for they dealt with the same facts, and they were moved by the same feelings. Among others

[1] Miscellany, p. 165.

who have spoken was Mrs. Eddy, the [Founder] of Christian Science. She issued two utterances which were read in her churches, one a communication on the death of the President, the other a letter of sympathy and advice to Mrs. McKinley. Both of these discourses are seemly and kind, but they are materially different from the writings of any one else. Reciting the praises of the dead President, Mrs. Eddy says: "May his history waken a tone of truth that shall reverberate, renew euphony, emphasize humane power, and bear its banner into the vast forever." No one else said anything like that. Mrs. Eddy's style is a personal asset. Her sentences usually have the considerable literary merit of being unexpected. Her letter to Mrs. McKinley was short, sympathetic, religious, and very much to the point. Her position in the country as the head and chief spokesman of an important religious body is very curious and highly interesting.

I once asked Mrs. Eddy if she had pursued some definite method, or had any special training, to attain her distinctive literary style. "None whatever," she responded, as I later recorded; "I have never given the subject any consideration; I have written as moved by the Spirit. I greatly dislike circumlocution and I always felt that a writer as well as a speaker should come at once to the point."

From many just estimates of Mrs. Eddy as a writer and author we take this quotation from a prominent daily newspaper:

The profound scholarship . . . that had penetrated the depths of the labyrinth of human knowledge may be accorded belated recognition. Men of letters . . . read the book[1] which in the artistry of its proportion, the felicity of its expression, the puissance of its logic, its rare grammatical purity, the splendor of its visions, and the sweetness of its message is, in simple truth, a book of books.[2]

[1] "Science and Health with Key to the Scriptures."
[2] Editorial Comments on the Life and Work of Mary Baker Eddy, p. 42.

Occasionally one hears the argument that the first edition of "Science and Health" expressed Mrs. Eddy's highest revelation, but she did not so consider it, and she makes it very plain on page 237 of "The First Church of Christ, Scientist, and Miscellany," that Christian Scientists should read her latest edition and not the ones in which printers had made mistakes or in which she had not presented her final thought. No more succinct illustration of this could be given than the following. When I told her that her student, Mrs. Mary W. Munroe, had sent her Christian Science library, including a copy of the first edition of "Science and Health," to the Concord church, Mrs. Eddy wrote me:

Beloved Student

I have requested your church to sell to me the first edition of Science and Health. . . .

I have not this edition and want it because I need it for *reference*. Besides it was spoiled by the publisher and it should not be in the minds of the students. Will you do me the favor of getting the church to send this book to me?

The Concord church gladly complied with Mrs. Eddy's request by making her a present of the first edition of the textbook.

Referring to the use of Science and Health in the Sunday Lesson-Sermon and the frequent quotations from it in the periodicals, Mrs. Eddy once wrote: "Did ever before a book stand the drain that [Science and Health] does and not get empty?"

Many of Mrs. Eddy's articles now found in her "Prose Works" appeared originally in the public press. When

[96]

in 1907 the *Cosmopolitan Magazine* asked Mrs. Eddy to contribute an article, she responded with "Youth and Young Manhood," now reprinted in "The First Church of Christ, Scientist, and Miscellany," page 272.

The editor of *The Boston Herald* at one time requested Mrs. Eddy, along with a number of prominent ministers, to give her favorite text and her reason for it. The result was the now well-known passage beginning, "The First Commandment is my favorite text." This vital statement met with a wide and cordial reception and Mrs. Eddy later incorporated it in the textbook, Science and Health, in which it now fittingly appears as the closing words of the chapter, "Science of Being" (p. 340).

Moved by inspiration, Mrs. Eddy expressed her thoughts in poetry with astonishing ease and rapidity. The remarkable poem "Christ and Christmas" was written in a very brief time. Desiring fitting illustrations for this poem, she needed an artist to work under her guidance, for she had formed a very definite concept of the message she wished the spiritually inspired illustrations to convey: that is, the coming of Christian Science, bringing salvation to the human race. To accomplish this it was necessary for her to have an artist who was willing to adapt his work to her ideas. This need was met by James F. Gilman, a Christian Scientist, who had recently come to live in Concord.

I had a very interesting visit with Mr. Gilman about the year 1901, when in speaking of himself he said that he had been a lone, hopeless wanderer, gifted with native ability for illustration, but he had become dissatisfied with his desultory art work. This was late in 1892, and he felt led by wisdom's call to leave his work and take up residence in Concord, New Hampshire, to devote himself to the study and practice of Christian Science. Although he had no definite opening in view, he departed for Concord in obedience solely to a divine intuition that it would be spiritually good for him to do so.

Soon after his arrival, he was engaged by a Concord photographer, who knew of his work, to make some sketches of Pleasant View. These sketches were made with Mrs. Eddy's permission. While he was engaged in this work, Mrs. Eddy commissioned him to aid her in making the illustrations for her poem, "Christ and Christmas." Thereafter he worked under her direct supervision until the illustrations were satisfactorily completed. Recognition of Mr. Gilman's work is recorded for all time in these words which appear in the printed copies of the poem, "Mary Baker Eddy and James F. Gilman, Artists."

Mary Baker Eddy was the sole founder of all the Christian Science periodicals. The establishment of these periodicals, which are the organs of the Christian Science movement, was a task which demanded her earnest thought, patience, and consecrated devotion. If she had accomplished nothing else in her lifetime than the launching of the quarterly, monthly, weekly, and daily periodicals from which Christian Scientists obtain so much inspiration, encouragement, and instruction, she would have done enough to deserve the everlasting love and gratitude of her followers.

As Mrs. Eddy advanced under God's guidance, in the founding of the Christian Science movement, every forward step cost her a struggle, for the carnal mind resisted every encroachment upon its age-old activities, every challenge to its tyranny. Over the infant Cause of Christian Science she faithfully watched as a mother watches over her babe. While others slept, Mrs. Eddy beheld grave dangers threatening the newborn Cause, and in the long night hours she asked God to give her the means of protecting that which had been entrusted to her care. As each Christian Science periodical appeared, including *The Christian Science Monitor*, it was not merely a journalistic or literary venture; it was a spiritual, life-dispensing message, designed to bring salvation to humanity, to serve as an entering wedge of release from mortality, from its terrors, agonies, despairs, and failures. It was designed to bring life to all; to enter into the history of each individual, to rehabilitate his experience, and to shape his destiny. As Mrs. Eddy prayed to be shown how best to bring this truth to humanity, the answer came to her. Periodicals would meet the need.

In the early days, Mrs. Eddy not only served as editor of *The Christian Science Journal*, the first periodical of the movement, which she established in 1883, but she contributed a large part of its contents. And incidentally, a good deal more than that. During the early years of the *Journal*, when it was a source of expense, Mrs. Eddy stood loyally by it, furnished a home for it, and bore the chief burden of its publication. The time soon came when the *Journal* had made for itself a place and a name, and commanded the respect and love of a greater constituency. Then Mrs. Eddy gave it to her followers.[1]

It was an inspiring experience for those associated with the Discoverer and Founder of Christian Science to see that no extremity daunted her. When unlooked-for opposition endeavored to upset the tiny craft of the new-born Cause, Mrs. Eddy, wise, forbearing, alert, guided it safely through stormy waters.

How great was the love she bore for every earnest seeker for the truth, whatever his human shortcomings! Despite the frequent disappointments which were hers, when her followers failed to measure up to her hopes and expectations, I can testify that her love and compassionate tenderness continued to guide all who would receive the blessing.

One of the marked characteristics of Christian Science is the universal appeal it has made to all races and nationalities. The prayer of Mrs. Eddy's German-speaking followers for a periodical in their own tongue was answered in April, 1903, when she founded *Der Herold der Christian Science*.

This periodical sprang into instant favor with German Christian Scientists, and they were especially pleased when its advertising pages were opened to practitioners

[1] Soon after The Mother Church, on the corner of Falmouth and Norway Streets, Boston, had been dedicated in January, 1895, it was announced that The Christian Science Publishing Society was to occupy its own building at 95 Falmouth Street. Within a year, 97 Falmouth Street was added to it. This was good news to Mrs. Eddy's followers. Two years later *The Christian Science Journal* for February, 1898, bore the glad news of Mrs. Eddy's conveyance in perpetuity to The First Church of Christ, Scientist, in Boston, Massachusetts, of all the real estate of The Christian Science Publishing Society, including the buildings located at 95–97 Falmouth Street, its money and assets, and all of its literary publications.

who spoke the German language. It also printed the Christian Science Bible Lessons in German, making the monthly indispensable to the German students.

Since the inauguration of *Der Herold der Christian Science* other *Heralds* have been launched where the need and the demand have been felt, until these foreign language publications of The Christian Science Publishing Society now include a French, a Scandinavian, and a Dutch *Herald*, in addition to the original German one.

Early in her experience Mary Baker Eddy found that before her lay a struggle to maintain the purity of her revelation. She saw that it was necessary that the truth of Christian Science should be expressed with the utmost clarity. The careful searching supervision which Mrs. Eddy constantly exercised over all the publications of the movement, I had ample opportunity to observe when, for a brief time, I served as associate editor of the Christian Science periodicals. The editors received from Mrs. Eddy a veritable university education in literary workmanship. She gave them both verbal and written instruction, revised their manuscripts, pointed out their mistakes, and lovingly rebuked their blunders. In the morning hours at Pleasant View, she could often be seen seated in her favorite rocker in her study, making frequent notations on the pad which she held in her lap. It was her practice to go over most carefully not only the editorials, but often the leading articles, in the *Journal* and *Sentinel*. As she scanned the columns of the Christian Science periodicals, rarely, if ever, did any mistake escape her notice.

Mrs. Eddy alone gave the name to each one of the Christian Science periodicals. She has said: "I have given the name to all the Christian Science periodicals. The first was *The Christian Science Journal,* designed to put on record the divine Science of Truth; the second I entitled *Sentinel,* intended to hold guard over Truth, Life, and Love; the third, *Der Herold der Christian Science,* to proclaim the universal activity and availability of Truth; the next I named *Monitor,* to spread undivided the Science that operates unspent. The object of the *Monitor* is to injure no man, but to bless all mankind."[1]

Her own writings Mrs. Eddy edited with painstaking care. Although the pressure of events at times demanded that she prepare her articles, poems, and other material with rapidity, they were most diligently revised. In those early days, therefore, if the periodicals were not always issued on the exact date, occasionally the reason was that at the last moment Mrs. Eddy saw an opportunity to clarify a statement in one of her articles. She would make the necessary corrections on the proofs submitted to her and send them from Pleasant View back to Boston, where the changes would be made in accordance with her directions and the presses started again. Precise in every detail, she insisted upon seeing the final proofs as well as the first proofs.

In the publication of her revisions of Science and Health, Mrs. Eddy exercised the closest supervision over every detail. The page proofs were given to her with her alterations marked in red pencil, then she carefully

[1] Miscellany, p. 353.

reviewed each point again, and either rejected or approved it separately.

Mr. John Wilson of the famous Cambridge publishing house, who for many years was Mrs. Eddy's printer, said to his workers, when a new book by her was coming from the press, "We must be very guarded, for if there is a single mistake in orthography or syntax Mrs. Eddy will detect it." At another time he declared that Mrs. Eddy was the writer most exact in diction, rhetoric, and punctuation of all the writers he had ever met. Her revisions of her textbook, Science and Health, were prompted by but one desire: that the statement of the truth might express God's revelation of Himself to mankind with complete accuracy and purity.

Speaking of the great difficulties she had encountered with regard to the second and third editions of "Science and Health," I recall that Mrs. Eddy said:

To publish the second edition of "Science and Health," I sought one of the leading firms of printers in Boston. When the book came from their hands I found so many mistakes that almost the entire edition which was printed in two volumes was spoiled, but the firm refused to reprint the book or make good in any way their fatal blunder. And there was no way to compel them, except through a lawsuit, a proposition I refused to entertain. I had exhausted all my available means and could not afford to publish the book anew, but the book as it came from the printers could not be circulated. While I was in the depths of this affliction and the burden seemed greater than I could bear, my husband, Asa G. Eddy, said to me, "There is now passing the house a gentleman, Mr. Wilson,[1] who I am confident can help you out of this dilemma. Shall I not speak to him?" I replied, "Please call him in." My husband at once spoke to him and Mr. Wilson gladly came in. I presented the

[1] Mr. John Wilson of the University Press, Cambridge, Massachusetts.

[103]

situation to him. He was amazed that the firm refused to make adequate reparation, but he told us of a plan whereby he believed that at least one of the volumes could be saved, and kindly offered to see the publisher in Boston. When the plan was presented to the firm, they consented to it. For this kindness Mr. Wilson made no charge.

Other trouble was in store for me, however. I had expended a large sum of money for the stereotype plates for the book and I looked forward to using these plates for the next edition with a new publisher. When I visited the firm to obtain the plates, I was calmly told that as soon as the former edition had been printed the plates had been melted up. I then appealed to Mr. Wilson to undertake the publication of the third edition of "Science and Health," which he was at first loath to do, as the book was so contrary to his religious convictions. But finally our good friend stepped into the breach and assumed its publication.

Mrs. Eddy's farseeing wisdom was nowhere more strikingly illustrated than in the founding of her daily newspaper. There had been much criticism of the sensational character of a large part of the daily press shortly prior to 1908. Not a few writers outlined in thought a truly Christian daily, and many futile attempts had been made to establish such a paper. Yet, in spite of protests, the daily press was largely growing more and more sensational and materialistic. Mrs. Eddy knew what divine wisdom required, and when the time was ripe she took the initial step for meeting that requirement by establishing her own newspaper.

A step was taken in that direction during the process of building The Mother Church Extension, when the property adjoining The Mother Church on the west side of St. Paul Street was acquired by the church. In 1907, the Field received the welcome news that a new and larger Publishing House was to be built, to meet the growing needs of The Christian Science Publishing Society. Mrs. Eddy's followers responded quickly and in July, 1908, a unit of the building was ready for occupancy. A long-cherished plan had been consummated, and the Publishing Society was in a beautiful new home of its own. All this building proceeded regardless of the financial panics of this period, proving Mrs. Eddy's premise of the infinite supply of Spirit.

If a temptation to rest on their oars now came to Boston workers, this thought was quickly dispelled by Mrs. Eddy's request for the immediate publication of a Christian Science daily newspaper. She approved the enlargement of the newly-built Publishing House to accommodate the presses and other machinery needed for the new daily paper. She also gave instructions as to the character and scope of the new publication.

When Mrs. Eddy discussed with some of her household the advisability of the publication of a daily newspaper, they very generally counseled against it. They spoke of the great expense, of the large number of employees necessary, and of her own burdens, which at her age seemed sufficient, without taking on additional ones. Her reply was, "God calls upon me to found a daily newspaper," and *The Christian Science Monitor* was founded.

I remember so well that thrilling occasion when Mrs. Eddy took her stand for the naming of *The Christian Science Monitor*. Some Christian Scientists were shaking their heads dubiously over the situation, the editors, members of the technical force, some of the members of Mrs.

Eddy's household, and others. It was secretly whispered about that greater success would attend the newspaper if the words "Christian Science" were omitted from the name. As a last resort, an interview was secured with Mrs. Eddy, at which time the editor-in-chief and the manager of the Publishing Society endeavored to win her to this view. The members of the household were on tiptoes, waiting outside the door of Mrs. Eddy's room, while the final decision was being made. The conference was brief. A moment or so, and the editor emerged. Said he, "Mrs. Eddy is firm, and her answer is, 'God gave me this name and it remains.'"

Although it was not to be a strictly religious paper in the ordinarily accepted meaning of the term, one article of a religious nature was to appear in each issue. I was with Mrs. Eddy at the time she gave directions for a religious article on Christian Science to be published each day on the Home Forum page. She chose the name Home Forum because she said she wished to appeal to the heart of the family circle. Several years prior to this, she had shown me her personal scrapbook, which was no doubt an inspiration to her for the Home Forum page, for it contained numerous carefully selected clippings from various newspapers and magazines.

It was an eventful day when the first test copy of *The Christian Science Monitor* was printed. That morning, Mrs. Eddy called the members of the household into her study. Seated at her desk, perusing with deepest interest the first copy of her great newspaper, she asked us if it were a dark morning. "Yes," replied one, "a heavy fog makes it darker than usual." Mr. Frye said that according to sense it was dark. Mrs. Eddy replied: "Yes, but only according to sense. We know the reverse of error is true. This, in truth, is the lightest day of all days. This is the day when our daily paper goes forth to lighten mankind . . . !"

Each day, a copy of the *Monitor* was sent to Mrs. Eddy, the religious article and each editorial being rubber stamped with the name of the writer, that she might know who wrote each important item. She read discriminatingly, critically, and appreciatively each article; if she had any comments, they were sent to the editor.

Mrs. Eddy approved of advertising in *The Christian Science Monitor*. This was evidenced on the occasion of the first appearance of a full-page advertisement of a Boston firm.[1] When it was brought to her attention, she was greatly pleased and requested a member of her household to convey to the firm her appreciation of the advertisement.

Very few, if any works which, in her marvelous career, Mrs. Eddy carried forth to pre-eminent success, were more commented on, more criticized, more debated by her followers and the public, than the purpose, motive, and contents of *The Christian Science Monitor* as a newspaper. Earnest but superficial critics had varied and contradictory notions of what the paper should be. They differed vigorously as to its contents, one group holding that since it was founded and supported by a religious

[1] Jordan Marsh Company had the first full-page advertisement in *The Christian Science Monitor* for January 11, 1909.

organization, it should be a religious publication rather than a newspaper. Even those who agreed that it was not to be a religious sheet, but a daily newspaper, had their vociferous differences. A pronounced section held that it should avoid local issues and give forth almost exclusively world-wide news. Just as determined was another group who fought for a paper largely given to the local news of Boston and New England, while world-wide news was to have secondary place.

What the character of its news was to be, also provoked vigorous discussions. One side held that nothing should be said about crime, or accidents, or war. Others declared that the paper should print the unvarnished story of the world's ills, however wretched and sordid might be the tale of disaster and calamity.

Mrs. Eddy was in no way shaken by the futile attempts of ignorance to snatch the paper from the divine order ordained by its founder. She was ever a warrior with armor on and sword in hand. Before the paper was in the printer's hands it was announced in an editorial in the *Christian Science Sentinel* for October 17, 1908, that *The Christian Science Monitor* was to be "a strictly up-to-date newspaper, in which all the news of the day that should be printed will find a place. . . ." And to this was added, "whose service will not be restricted to any one locality or section, but will cover the daily activities of the entire world."

Another point emphasized in the *Sentinel* announcement of October 17, 1908, was that "the *Monitor* shall contain, in addition to the usual news feature of the best city papers, such special departments as will make it a home paper of the highest grade,—one which will appeal to good men and women everywhere. . . ."

In conclusion, an editorial in the November 14, 1908, *Sentinel* frankly stated, "To those who have inquired whether the *Monitor* is to be a real newspaper, we say, Yes. To those who have asked whether it will be 'simply a Boston newspaper,' we say, No, except that a special New England edition, which will give the current local news of that section, is to be issued each day."

Mrs. Eddy's thought of *The Christian Science Monitor*, as I learned from her, is well expressed in its issue of September 4, 1934:

> The essential function of a newspaper is to print the news. It is the desire and determination of the Monitor today to record and interpret, in true perspective, all of the world's significant news. The test of all Monitor news is whether that news is socially important, whether it is news which we all need to know in order to be informed and alert citizens. It is the goal of the Monitor to give to its readers a newspaper which will be vital, realistic and comprehensive, which will give to the good news, to the encouraging news and to the constructive news the prominence it rightfully deserves. At the same time the Monitor ignores nothing essential to a penetrating understanding of those aggravated social conditions to which readers of the Monitor, particularly, can give healing attention.

The editorial page of the same issue of the *Monitor* declared: "Today the world is faced with increasingly challenging conditions which need to be recorded 'in completeness sufficient for information' and which need to be understood in order to be corrected." As at its founding, the *Monitor* today sets for itself that goal.

To insure that every publication issuing from The Christian Science Publishing Society should be "ably edited and kept abreast of the times," Mrs. Eddy established a By-Law to that effect.[1] In Mrs. Eddy's desire to share with all the blessings of Christian Science, she provided through the Church Manual for the establishment of free Reading Rooms, where the investigator may have access to the unadulterated statement of Christian Science through the authorized literature of the movement.

Essentially a giver, not a getter, no one was a more liberal distributor of her book, Science and Health, and of her other writings, than was their author. Indeed, she was the first Distribution Committee of Christian Science. During my association with her, she had a long list of friends to whom she distributed, not only her books, but copies of the Christian Science periodicals and important articles relating to Christian Science. At her direction, a Distribution Committee was formed in the Concord church; it met regularly and sent such articles as were approved to the legislators and other prominent persons in her home state of New Hampshire.

Any examination of Mrs. Eddy's activities as an author must of necessity be inadequate. The mere recounting of the facts can never tell of the earnest labor, of the consecrated prayer which she gave to the preparation of her monumental works. Up to the time of closing her College, in a single day she often taught a class, interviewed students, settled knotty church problems, and then, while others were sleeping, wrote far into the night, laboring

[1] Church Manual, p. 44.

[110]

long and arduously to give the precise interpretation of God's Word which might be needed to convince the reader of the truth of Christian Science. Early the next morning she would be at her desk, dictating to her secretary the stirring words of some one of her works before the gathering of the class.

Stopping to call one afternoon on her drive in Concord, New Hampshire, she told me that she had been at work the night before until four o'clock in the morning. After all this labor, to her fell the task of correcting the mistakes of typists, printers, and proofreaders. How little the world knows, how slightly it appreciates, the hardships and the self-sacrifice of Mary Baker Eddy in presenting her inspired revelation to the sons of men! Only through divine wisdom and unceasing toil did she accomplish the work of keeping Christian Science unadulterated. What humanity owes to her foresight in establishing The Christian Science Publishing Society, it now little comprehends, but future ages will accord a just estimate to the untiring labor and manifold achievements of the Founder of the Christian Science movement.

CHAPTER VII

IT has often been asked, Why did Mary Baker Eddy found a separate denomination? Why did she not remain in the old church and help it with whatever good she had discovered?

Originally Mrs. Eddy had no plans for establishing a new denomination, for, as I heard her say many times, she confidently expected that the Christian church would welcome her discovery and adopt the healing ministry as an integral part of its activity, even as the early church for three centuries after the resurrection had utilized spiritual means to heal the sick. Indeed, some of her early students spoke in their own prayer meetings of their increased faith in the efficacy of prayer to heal the sick as well as the sinning. But these members frequently were informed by the officers of their churches that such testimony was not welcome, and were advised not to indulge in such blasphemy.

The reception which her discovery encountered in the church was not foreseen by Mrs. Eddy, for she had hopefully looked forward to its immediate acceptance, as is seen by her own words: "Until the author of this book learned the vastness of Christian Science, the fixedness of mortal illusions, and the human hatred of Truth, she cherished sanguine hopes that Christian Science would meet with immediate and universal acceptance."[1]

[1] Science and Health, p. 330.

[112]

But this "universal acceptance" did not occur; so the healing of Christ Jesus again came unto its own, but its own received it not. The orthodox church was not ready to restore healing to its ministry.

It was only natural, then, that Mrs. Eddy and her followers should seek to have a church of their own which would permit them to re-establish Jesus' healing ministry by doing his works. At first a small group of students met in the parlors of some of its members. This continued for several years. With increased growth and the inconvenience of going from one house to another, the need for an organized church and a centrally located meeting place became apparent. This resulted in the establishment in Boston, in August, 1879, of the Church of Christ, Scientist, under a Massachusetts State charter, whose purpose it was to "reinstate primitive Christianity and its lost element of healing."[1] That same month twenty-six of its members extended a call to Mary Baker Eddy to become their pastor.

First C. S. Church established Aug 1879

As the church prospered, it encountered difficulties. Some of her students became dissatisfied and went their own way. One early student told me that at one time while calling on Mrs. Eddy at her Commonwealth Avenue home, she found her much depressed. "Whom can I count as faithful?" she asked. "My dear," her student replied, "you have more faithful disciples than the Master had." Mrs. Eddy then remarked, "I thank you indeed for your rebuke. I have much for which to be grateful."

The importance of eliminating the continuance of the

[1] Church Manual, p. 17.

discordant conditions became more and more apparent to Mrs. Eddy, and she promptly set to work to remedy them. The final step in this direction resulted in the dissolution of the material form of church organization as it was then constituted. She knew that the real church, which was so clearly defined in her own consciousness, must also come in the hearts and minds of her followers before it could be manifested.

This is her inspired concept of what properly constitutes the true church and its functions:

CHURCH. The structure of Truth and Love; whatever rests upon and proceeds from divine Principle.

The Church is that institution, which affords proof of its utility and is found elevating the race, rousing the dormant understanding from material beliefs to the apprehension of spiritual ideas and the demonstration of divine Science, thereby casting out devils, or error, and healing the sick.[1]

While contemplating this final change, Mrs. Eddy left Boston and sought the more secluded environment of Concord, New Hampshire. Far from withdrawing from active service, however, she was instead as busily engaged as she had been in her whole life. Watching over a Cause that held within its care the welfare of mankind, she continued to seek the guidance of the one Mind. Now the dismantling of the organization which she had for years been laboring to build up took place. Not only was the church organization in its existing form dissolved, but she also closed the Massachusetts Metaphysical College. God had revealed to her, she said, that a church of the Spirit must have a spiritual foundation.

[1] Science and Health, p. 583.

Over this true church the Founder prayed long and earnestly. "I knew that to God's gift, foundation and superstructure," she wrote, "no one could hold a wholly material title."[1] In the year 1892, therefore, she reorganized the church, establishing it on the basis upon which it now rests.

The difficulties and obstructions she encountered during this process were numerous and severe. Nevertheless, persuaded within herself that she was divinely led, the Founder stood her ground until at length the organization of the new church was found to be completely sanctioned and protected by law. Relating the circumstances of this unfoldment, Mrs. Eddy said to me at one time:

When the Boston attorneys failed to find a law by which our church could obtain a charter, I called in the services of the Hon. Reuben Walker, now Judge of the Supreme Court of the State of New Hampshire. I asked him to find for us a law to fit the case. He said that he knew of no such law upon the statute books. I asked him upon what was human law based. He reflected and then said, "Upon the divine law. But," he said, "if the Massachusetts abstracter of law can find no such statute, how can I?" To this I replied, "God has somewhere provided such a law and I know you can find it."

Three days later my secretary visited him, and found him lost in a pile of law books he had been examining. His greeting was, "I have found the law." It was a statute which was enacted to suit the needs of the Methodist Church, and fully met our requirements.[2]

She proved that what God wills, no human law or power can impede or oppose.

In establishing First Church of Christ, Scientist, of

[1] "Miscellaneous Writings," p. 140.
[2] See footnote, Church Manual, p. 130.

[115]

Concord, New Hampshire, Mrs. Eddy made plain to me the difference between the government of The Mother Church and that of its branch churches. She explained that the government of The Mother Church in Boston is unique, since all its transactions are authorized by the Manual of The Mother Church, which stands as an example of the highest form of spiritual government. The conduct of its activities rests with the one Mind, God. The Manual of The Mother Church was given to her followers by Mary Baker Eddy through divine inspiration to be the governing law of the Christian Science movement.

The Christian Science Board of Directors is primarily enjoined under the Church Manual to safeguard the spiritual welfare of The Mother Church. In addition, the Directors, seeking God's direction and guidance, elect all the officers, fill all vacancies, and conduct all the affairs of The Mother Church. Thus, they select the Readers for the church, safeguard all funds, provide for the management of all real estate of The Mother Church, the erection of needed buildings, and see that all the affairs of the church and its trusteeships and administrative activities are conducted in accordance with the Manual.

The members of branch Churches of Christ, Scientist, however, entrust the business affairs of their churches to Boards of Trustees or Directors whom they elect, and to whom certain duties are delegated. The entire government of the branch churches is thus conducted on a democratic basis. The branch churches seek to demonstrate unity through realizing, and witnessing to, the government of the one Mind, and as authorized branches they are at one with The Mother Church. The unity of the movement which is maintained by the provision whereby members of branch churches may become members of The Mother Church is proclaimed in our Leader's potent words:

> The Magna Charta of Christian Science means much, *multum in parvo,*—all-in-one and one-in-all. It stands for the inalienable, universal rights of men. Essentially democratic, its government is administered by the common consent of the governed, wherein and whereby man governed by his creator is self-governed.[1]

Mrs. Eddy often spoke of her experience in supervising the remodeling of the colonial mansion in Concord, which she gave to the Concord Scientists as their first church home. After discussing her plan for remodeling the house with one of Concord's best builders, she engaged him to carry on the work. She wrote of this experience:

> He drew the plan, showed it to me, and I accepted it. From that time, October 29, 1897, until the remodelling of the house was finished, I inspected the work every day, suggested the details outside and inside from the foundations to the tower, and saw them carried out. One day the carpenters' foreman said to me: "I want to be let off for a few days. I do not feel able to keep about. I am feeling an old ailment my mother had." I healed him on the spot. He remained at work, and the next morning said to Mr. George H. Moore of Concord, "I am as well as I ever was."[2]

Mrs. Eddy took an affectionate satisfaction in associating Christian Science Hall with the very early days when her parents attended the North Congregational Church in Concord. In a message which she sent to the

[1] Miscellany, pp. 246, 247.   [2] Miscellany, p. 145.

little group of Christian Scientists at the second Sunday service in the hall, on the twelfth of December, 1897, she wrote:

> There are moments when at the touch of memory the past comes forth like a pageant and the present is prophetic. Over a half century ago, between the morning and afternoon services of the First Congregational Church, the grand old elm on North State Street flung its foliage in kindly shelter over my childhood's Sunday noons. And now, at this distant day, I have provided for you a modest hall, in which to assemble as a sort of Christian Science kindergarten for teaching the "new tongue" of the gospel with "signs following," of which St. Mark prophesies.
>
> May this little sanctum be preserved sacred to the memory of this pure purpose, and subserve it.[1]

And in her first annual message, she expressed her tender love for the little flock:

> May this dear little church, nestled so near my heart and native hills, be steadfast in Christ, always abounding in love and good works, having unfaltering faith in the prophecies, promises, and proofs of Holy Writ.[2]

Christian Science Hall will ever occupy a sacred spot in the memory of Christian Scientists who value familiar landmarks in the history of the movement, for it was in this little sanctum that Mrs. Eddy taught her last class in 1898. And it was here, on occasions, that she met members of her Boston church. Over the entrance of the hall, Mrs. Eddy had directed that the following verse be inscribed, which she selected from an old hymn:

> Daughter of Zion, awake from thy sadness,
> Awake! for thy foes shall oppress thee no more!
> Bright o'er the hills dawns the day-star of gladness,
> Arise! for the night of thy sorrow is o'er.

[1] Miscellany, p. 147.   [2] Miscellany, p. 155.

Christian Science Hall

" 'I have provided for you a modest hall' "

Under the influence of Mrs. Eddy's presence in Concord, the church grew and the healing work prospered. It was in 1899, when the little society was holding its meetings in Christian Science Hall, that my sister Mary and I were called by Mrs. Eddy to serve as Readers there.

In February, 1899, persuaded that the time was ripe for the formation of a church in Concord, Mrs. Eddy requested me to take the necessary steps to form such an organization. In consultation with some of Mrs. Eddy's oldest and most loyal students in Boston, therefore, By-Laws were prepared for the new church. These By-Laws entrusted the conduct and management of the affairs of the church to a Board of Trustees, who were to elect the Readers, choose the lecturers, fill all vacancies in church offices, and conduct the general business of the church. Little if anything was left to be done by the church members.

That I should attempt in collaboration with Mrs. Eddy's leading students to form such By-Laws showed how little comprehension workers had in the year 1899 of the meaning of democracy in Christian Science. When I gave the By-Laws to Mrs. Eddy for her criticism, she returned them, saying they were not suitable for a branch church, for they copied the By-Laws of The Mother Church, and the government of The Mother Church could not be considered a model for a branch church. In accordance with her recommendation, a copy of the By-Laws of a democratic branch church was secured to serve as a model for the Concord church. New By-Laws were then formed, which placed the affairs of the church in the hands of its members, who were to elect the Trustees, and decide all important questions affecting the branch church. The Trustees were to look after the business of the church in the interim between church membership meetings, but the church, as Mrs. Eddy desired it, was to be a democratic institution. When these new By-Laws were submitted to Mrs. Eddy, she gave them her endorsement.

That all Christian Scientists might clearly understand her desire that branch churches shall be truly democratic in their government, Mrs. Eddy published a By-Law which reads in part:

> In Christian Science each branch church shall be distinctly democratic in its government, and no individual, and no other church shall interfere with its affairs.[1]

From the moment of the organization of the Concord church, Christian Scientists in the Field at large showed a deep interest in its welfare. They made occasional trips to Concord to attend its services and gave generous contributions. When Mrs. Eddy was asked to head the list of charter members, she graciously declined, for she had made it clear that she wished the members of a branch church to conduct its own affairs.

It was in 1903, when the congregation had outgrown Christian Science Hall, that Mrs. Eddy began the work of building a church edifice on the site of the hall. To aid her in the work, she appointed a financial committee of three. In February, 1903, she wrote to me:

[1] Church Manual, p. 74.

Look up a straight, capable, smart man to put on our building Com. and let us have our church built. The Hall looks shabby.

Later she wrote:

I greatly desire to start work on the new church in Concord soon and you can talk with Mr. Frye on that subject when he has time.

On July 16, 1903, she wrote me as follows:

My soul, sense, doth magnify the Lord. I have seen of the *travail* of my *soul* and rejoice. Yes, I am satisfied now with your arrangement and can, shall, take you all in the arms of faith and offer you anew to our God, and He will baptize you in the flood of His love and your hearts, and not pride will consecrate this temple from its foundation to Him who will build our bodies sacred temples pure and eternal.

On the same day she sent me the following message at one o'clock:

The sacred hour of prayer is past. God grant us the desire that this Temple be His forever.

Mrs. Eddy's deep interest in the minutest details of the progress of the Cause in Concord, her home city, is indicated by the above and numerous other letters written to me while the building of the Concord church was progressing. Her gifts to her Concord followers included about twenty thousand dollars which she expended for Christian Science Hall, the land on which it stood, and one hundred thousand dollars for the building of the new church.

As soon as it became known that Mrs. Eddy's gift of one hundred thousand dollars for the Concord church was to be used in its immediate erection, her followers in this country and abroad asked permission to join with her in supplying the funds for building a beautiful granite edifice. Money began to flow in from all parts of America, from the Atlantic to the Pacific, Christian Scientists in England and France also making generous contributions. These gifts, large and small, ranging from the "widow's mite" to the sum of ten thousand dollars contributed by a group of members of The Mother Church to provide an organ, showed the love of her followers for their Leader and for the church in her home city.

When, in the summer of 1904, the church was completed and plans were made to dedicate it on the seventeenth of July, Mrs. Eddy sent me the following letter:

> Something like this read at the close of each service tomorrow. That I, not having the time to receive all the beloved ones who have so kindly come to the dedication of this church,—I must not allow myself the pleasure of receiving any [one] of them. I always try to be just, if not generous; and I cannot show my love for them in social ways without neglecting the sacred demands on my time and attention for labors which I think do them more good.

The manifold activities of the Christian Science church which Mary Baker Eddy founded are a monument to her spoken words, "Things are thoughts that expressed take root," for the church organization and all the activities of the Christian Science movement first had their origin in Mrs. Eddy's thought, as the reflection of divine Mind.

"Our Cause is immortal," she once wrote to me, "it rests on nothing temporal, it is the cause and effect of all that really exists. What more is left us to desire than its acknowledgment and the unfolding of *God,* infinite Life, Love!"

First Church of Christ, Scientist, in Concord, New Hampshire

" 'God grant . . . that this Temple be His forever' "

CHAPTER VIII

THE general popular and too frequent concept of a leader of any important movement or undertaking is a man or woman of strong personality, physical vigor, inflexible will, plus a self-confident conviction of his or her own ability. In addition to possessing these characteristics, a leader is often credited with a desire to control others, exact a blind submission from his or her followers, and to bask in the sunshine of their servile adulation.

Mrs. Eddy's inspired leadership, however, was based on a loving, wholehearted desire to lead her followers to a greater spiritual understanding of Truth, *not* to a sickly devotion to her own personality. In convincing confirmation of this she says in ringing tones in her Message to The Mother Church for 1902 (p. 4), "I again repeat, Follow your Leader, only so far as she follows Christ."

Mary Baker Eddy sought no control over others, no supine submission to her will, no sycophantic obsequiousness. Although well aware of the spiritual value of affection and gratitude, there were times when Mrs. Eddy felt compelled to rebuke some of her followers for undue contemplation of her personality, and in a remarkable article called "Personal Contagion" in "The First Church of Christ, Scientist, and Miscellany" (p. 116), she says: "In time of religious or scientific prosperity, certain individuals are inclined to cling to the personality of its leader. This state of mind is sickly; it is a contagion—a mental malady, which must be met and overcome. Why? Because it would dethrone the First Commandment, Thou shalt have one God."

Mrs. Eddy's leadership was a God-inspired leadership. She knew that spiritual power is derived from humility and that in order to qualify as a true leader of mankind one must first qualify as a follower of God.

Those of us who were closely associated with Mary Baker Eddy over a period of years could not fail to realize how well equipped she was for her position as Leader of the Christian Science movement. When at one time it was related to her that at a Wednesday night meeting in The Mother Church a speaker had said, "Mrs. Eddy is a leader because she permits God to lead her," I was told she very simply responded:

I have not sought leadership. Before the great problems that have been given to me, I have felt myself nothing. There has been a voice saying to me, "Mary, take yourself out of the way and let God act through you."

On another occasion when a difficult problem connected with a branch church had been solved harmoniously, a member of the household thanked Mrs. Eddy for her "love, wisdom, and bravery" during the troublous times just past. Quietly Mrs. Eddy was said to have replied:

I can try to unself Mary. I can try to enter into the place of a little child, to know that God has done it. This victory over error in the church will be a lesson for the whole Cause. All will be blessed by it.

That same humility and self-abnegation shone through her words of counsel to her followers in 1899, when she wrote:

Lean not too much on your Leader. Trust God to direct your steps. Accept my counsel and' teachings only as they include the spirit and the letter of the Ten Commandments, the Beatitudes, and the teachings and example of Christ Jesus.[1]

Disclaiming personal leadership, this unusual woman sought to turn her followers to God, to whom she invariably looked for guidance and inspiration.

She wrote the following letter which gave joy and comfort to an early student:

I feel that you all have in my book *Science and Health* the anchor of your being that will prove sure and steadfast in storm and shine. O! how thankful I am that God has enabled me to give to you, my dear children in Christ, a rich inheritance.

Before taking any step in the founding of the Christian Science movement, Mrs. Eddy always sought the guidance of the one Mind. But after these periods of prayer and communion, she spoke as one who could not be swerved from a holy purpose. Having heard the divine voice, she obeyed implicitly.

Exploring a path so new and untried, Mrs. Eddy found she must train and instruct those who would follow in her footsteps. They must be taught to put off the old and adopt the new, as their thought advanced from a material sense to the spiritual. Her wise schooling guided the early footsteps of many a grateful student. Patiently and painstakingly, she instructed the officers and workers

[1] Miscellany, p. 129.

in the Cause, so that they were properly prepared for their special duties. It was natural that the greatest devotion and self-sacrifice should be expected of her followers, for only through such qualities could the Cause be established. Every quality she deemed essential to the Christian warfare, and demanded in her followers, she exemplified in her own life. In the conduct of her daily activities she lived the proverb, "Order is heaven's first law," and she expected her church, its officers, and its members, to observe the same orderly procedure in the discharge of their official duties and in the conduct of their lives. To the task of establishing the healing truth she was wholeheartedly consecrated. She had no other concern. She never took a vacation, never spent time in social diversion, but devoted herself entirely to her Cause. At one time, according to my remembrance, she said:

> I left home and friends, and I gave up a large income as a writer, in order to serve the Cause of Christian Science. I have endured in its behalf all shame and blame and I have lived these down. This is the experience of your Leader. Are her followers willing to take up their crosses as she has taken up hers, in order to follow Christ, or do they demand all that they want for doing it, or otherwise leave their Leader and the Cause? Let all Christian Scientists who come to help their Leader answer this question to their God. Otherwise, let them refuse to come, and give their reply accordingly.

Prayerfully pondering the needs of the moment, Mrs. Eddy had early found that a vigorous organization, made up of active growing parts, requires a proper form of government to control its activities. Only one who turned to God for inspiration, guidance, and wisdom would have seen the necessity for a proper means of control of this organization. Only one obedient to the divine command would have had the courage to institute such a directive. Mrs. Eddy provided in the Manual of The Mother Church a God-given instrument which more than once has proved its value as a protection against ill-advised tendencies and faulty growth in the movement.

The Manual of The Mother Church was born of necessity. Mrs. Eddy never expected, at first, that it would be needful to give Christian Scientists rules for conduct, as she once said in conversation something to this effect:

> When I began my church, I said to one of my students, "This church shall be different from all other churches, for it shall have no By-Laws." But before the first year had passed, the exigencies of the case demanded that certain rules should be adopted for church government. Thus came the Church Rules and By-Laws.

The Rules and By-Laws of the Church Manual were written at different periods, as varying human demands of the organization arose. Only as the result of her spiritual communion with God was each By-Law given to the world. Once she spoke to me of a solution she had in mind to meet a trying situation and added, "But God had a better plan and would not let me have my way." She knew that God, divine Mind, must speak and be obeyed, to have His Cause established on earth. After her long nights of vigil, of unseen silent communion with her heavenly Father, Mrs. Eddy felt convinced of the divine origin of the Church By-Laws, so that she later wrote of them:

Of this I am sure, that each Rule and By-law in this Manual will increase the spirituality of him who obeys it, invigorate his capacity to heal the sick, to comfort such as mourn, and to awaken the sinner.[1]

So certain was she of this conviction, that she caused the final By-Law to read:

No new Tenet or By-Law shall be adopted, nor any Tenet or By-Law amended or annulled, without the written consent of Mary Baker Eddy, the author of our textbook, SCIENCE AND HEALTH.[2]

A clear understanding of its origin and unfoldment enables one to discern why loyal Christian Scientists have always regarded the Church Manual as of vital importance to the Cause. Mrs. Eddy often intimated that in the work of establishing Christian Science upon a sound and scientific basis, the Manual of The Mother Church is second in importance only to the textbook, "Science and Health with Key to the Scriptures."

In organizing her church in 1892, Mrs. Eddy discerned the need of creating by a Deed of Trust a governing Board to be known as The Christian Science Board of Directors which should be vested with authority to direct the activities of the movement. This step taken, she was further led by divine wisdom to provide for their proper functioning and guidance under a Church Manual which commissions this Board to enforce and effectively carry out its every provision. Thus the Board's actions are subject to the Church Manual, which is the supreme authority of the Christian Science church.

By these wise provisions in the ordination of the Church

[1] Miscellany, p. 230.   [2] Church Manual, p. 105.

Manual and the governing Board of The Mother Church, its Christian Science Board of Directors, Mrs. Eddy guarded against one of the most prevalent errors of our times, namely, rebellion against constituted authority.

While Mrs. Eddy was at the helm, *The Christian Science Journal* for May, 1885, printed this unsigned article which seems of special significance at this time:

> Earthly thrones tremble on their bases in these days of rebellion against despotism. It would seem as if the kingdoms of the world were all being weighed in balances to determine what boasted strength is real and what pretended. No ruler is sure of his foothold in any land. . . . All these rumblings of discord, to the watchers on Mount Zion, come fraught with assurance of the onward march of Righteousness. Whether the people recognize the presence or not it is here, making for their freedom. And not the dominion of acknowledged kings and princes alone is threatened—but the dominion of man over man in any form must give way to the liberty, fraternity and equality, toward which the unseen Law, spiritual and eternal, forces humanity.

Under Mrs. Eddy's wise guidance, the Christian Science organization has been, and is, marching forward toward "liberty, fraternity and equality."

CHAPTER IX

IN her loving desire to present pure Christian Science to the world through every possible legitimate channel, it was natural that Mrs. Eddy discerned in the early days of the movement that much good could be accomplished through preaching and lecturing. And, needless to say, Mary Baker Eddy herself was the first Christian Science lecturer.

Lecturing was nothing new to Mrs. Eddy. Long before her discovery of Christian Science she had delivered numerous addresses on various topics. In 1862, she lectured at Colby University, Waterville, Maine, on "The South and the North," and two years later she made a speech in Town Hall, Warren, Maine, against spiritualism. Also, Mrs. Eddy tells us on page 40 of "Retrospection and Introspection" that she "was called to speak before the Lyceum Club, at Westerly, Rhode Island." I have in my possession a quaintly worded card on which is printed the following notice of lectures to be delivered by Mrs. Eddy:

Invitation. Mary B. Glover Eddy, author of "Science and Health," will interest all who may favor her with a call at her rooms with her Parlor Lectures on Practical Metaphysics, and the influence that mind holds over disease and longevity.

How to improve the moral and physical condition of man to eradicate in children hereditary taints, to enlarge the intellect a hundred per cent, to restore and strengthen memory, to cure consumption, rheumatism, deafness, blindness and every ill the race is heir to. Place, College Rooms Columbus Ave. 569 Time, Thursday 3 P. M. Price $0.25 ·

While recalling the story of these lectures of long ago, Mrs. Eddy once said to me, as I later recorded her words:

In the early days of Christian Science, in order to interest people, I was forced to adopt many ways and methods. I would lecture to a parlor full of people and at the conclusion of the address, they would seem to grasp little, if anything. One evening, after speaking for a few moments, I asked all to rise who understood what I had been saying, and not one rose to his feet.

Later, when the Christian Scientist Association was formed, Mrs. Eddy frequently spoke at the meetings, which greatly inspired and strengthened the growing band of workers.

On one occasion, Mrs. Eddy said to a member of her household that the way to establish the Cause through reason is through writing and preaching, teaching and lecturing. This is temporal. But the way to establish the Cause through revelation is by healing, and this is permanent.

It was not until February, 1898, that Mrs. Eddy announced, through *The Christian Science Journal,* the appointment of a Christian Science Board of Lectureship. At first there was hesitation on the part of a few to accept this innovation. Not all of the branch churches were awake either to the need for lectures or to the value of printing them. And it was only through Mrs. Eddy's specific directions to the lecturers and her loving recommendations to the Field published in our periodicals, that the unique value of the Board of Lectureship was fully realized.

Mrs. Eddy, by private counsel, personal letters, articles in the periodicals, and through her By-Laws, prescribed charity and love to guide each member of The Christian Science Board of Lectureship. She demanded a high standard of these messengers of Christian Science, reminding them always that their God-inspired purpose was to "subserve the interest of mankind."[1]

On February 14, 1898, I was privileged to deliver, at Odd Fellows Hall, East Lynn, Massachusetts, the first lecture by a member of the Board of Lectureship. Among my cherished possessions is the following inspiring message received at that time from Mrs. Eddy:

I was glad to know you were called to the Bethlehem of Mass. and am waiting to hear from you again on this subject so near my heart.

The first called to lecture on the basis of the Lectureship and to one of the most important fields in the vineyard of our God!

Well it is ominous, full of promise. Once that city resounded with my cures. But if there is a hope eternal I feel it. God bless you, prosper the seed you sow. . . .

In those early days of the Board of Lectureship the present practice of delivering the same lecture to various parts of the Field had not been inaugurated, but early in September, 1898, Mrs. Eddy sent me a message with the following recommendation:

I suggest that you prepare a lecture with a view to giving it to the reporters and so make one answer for several places. Take the questions uppermost in the public mind and answer them systematically in Science.

[1] Miscellany, p. 339.

And shortly after that, on September 28, 1898, the privilege was mine to deliver the first lecture in the original edifice of The Mother Church. *[margin note: 1st mother Church lecture]*

Mrs. Eddy kept in close touch with the activities of the Board of Lectureship, and its members found her admonition and encouragement a constant source of inspiration. During my term of lectureship I was frequently greatly blessed by Mrs. Eddy's wise counsel and help. When a new lecture was submitted for her consideration, she never failed to give some word of encouragement or criticism.

I received this helpful note from Mrs. Eddy, which shows her solicitude for the heart qualities of a lecture: *[margin note: heart in lectures]*

Dear one, cultivate this tender emotion, have a cell less in the brain and a fibre more in the heart in yourself and it will do much for your lectures and in healing the sick. . . . When lecturing, or addressing the church . . . let this tenderness *appear* and like the dew, it will refresh the parched ear and lonely heart.

Through a By-Law, Mrs. Eddy made provision that every lecture shall "bear testimony to the facts pertaining to the life of the Pastor Emeritus."[1] The care which must be exercised in giving these facts was indicated, however, when she wrote me on February 21, 1898: " . . . do not I beg ever again speak so much in my praise. I feel so unworthy to be spoken of only as a humble servant of our God."

Mrs. Eddy indicated the loving manner in which misconceptions concerning Christian Science might be corrected when she wrote me as follows:

[1] Church Manual, Art. XXXI, Sect. 2.

. . . Be careful and not berate any religion; be charitable towards all men. Make your strong point showing the practical excellence of Christian Science. Arm yourself with divine Love then when you are "lifted up" you "will draw *all men*" *unto you.*

Mrs. Eddy saw the necessity at times of aiding the members of the Board of Lectureship in the presentation of their message. She knew that not words, but the realization of the truth behind them, was the power that enlightened and healed the multitude. Accordingly she wrote as follows to two lecturers:

My dear Students:

Mother must give you a lesson on mind of a few sentences. A real Metaphysician knows that Mind is the all and only power and the mental word inaudible more effective as a rule than the audible. Can you shelf this rule and be consistent? Do you heal the sick by physical or audible means?

Do you ever think speak act—by reason of matter or mind? Do you declare all this affirmatively in your lectures? Then does right and the demonstration thereof depend on matter or *mind?* If the latter how are you going to act rightly and cause others to do likewise most efficiently? Is it through mind-power and how? Orally or the "still, small voice" I beg you will demonstrate *our God* in Science as the *Principle* that *moves man's actions.* . . . *Think* before you act and your thoughts will govern yours and other men's lives more than your acts can.

It is beyond all question true that the pronounced success of The Christian Science Board of Lectureship from the time of its inception is largely due to the alertness, inspiration, and instruction of the first lecturer on Christian Science, Mary Baker Eddy.

With consummate wisdom Mrs. Eddy did not immediately cast aside all of the outward forms of practice of the old church in the early days when she was establishing the Cause of Christian Science. Her followers must be led step by step from a material to a spiritual basis of thought and action. At the outset, preaching was a part of the Christian Science Sunday service, and occasionally Christian Scientists were invited to speak from the pulpit of their former churches. Mrs. Eddy herself, of course, was the first Christian Science preacher.

Even before the revelation of Christian Science had come to her, Mrs. Eddy had taken an active part in the church of which she was a member. She had frequently responded to the request to offer prayer in public, and had presided at midweek prayer meetings. Now she became more eloquent than ever in praise of God.

After some years of teaching Christian Science and holding meetings for her followers in Lynn, Mrs. Eddy was led in 1878 to carry this new-old spiritual truth to Boston. Here she preached at the Baptist Tabernacle by invitation of its pastor. The congregation so increased in size that the pews were not adequate to seat the audience, and benches were used in the aisles. At the close of her engagement, many persons publicly testified to the healings they had experienced through her preaching.

The following year Mrs. Eddy and her followers organized a church under a Massachusetts State charter, and she became its pastor. Two years later she was ordained as such by her church. Concerning those early years she wrote:

. . . I preached four years, and built up the church, before I would accept the slightest remuneration. When the church had sufficient members and means to pay a salary, and refused to give me up or to receive my gratuitous services, I accepted, for a time, fifteen dollars each Sunday when I preached. I never received more than this; and the contributions, when I preached, doubled that amount.[1]

On Sundays she delivered her inspiring sermons to her church and the congregation grew until it overflowed into the aisles and numbers were turned away. Many whose privilege it was to hear this divinely inspired woman have given convincing evidence of her healing ministry.

That she never lost her great gift of eloquence in after years I am able to testify, for it was my privilege on February 26, 1898, to hear Mrs. Eddy deliver a remarkably inspiring address in Christian Science Hall, Concord, New Hampshire. At her invitation, a party of First Members of The Mother Church, nearly forty of us in number, were present in the attractive audience room of Christian Science Hall. Every inch of standing room on this historic occasion was taken and many were turned away. Among those present, besides the invited guests from Boston, New York, Philadelphia, Providence, Montreal, and the local congregation, were a number of non-Scientists, including the Mayor, the Postmaster, businessmen, lawyers, and editors of Concord papers.

After the preliminary exercises were conducted by the First Reader, Mr. Ezra M. Buswell, C. S. D., Mrs. Eddy appeared. As she entered the hall the entire audience by common impulse arose and remained standing until

[1] "Miscellaneous Writings," p. 349.

she had taken her place. At that date Mrs. Eddy was in her seventy-seventh year, yet except for her white hair there was no trace of age in her appearance, manner, gesture, or voice. The *Concord Evening Monitor* of February 27, 1898, in its account said, "Mrs. Eddy appeared at her best, as sprightly and energetic as a young woman."

She took the ninety-first Psalm as the subject of her address, reading the Scriptures without glasses. Speaking for three quarters of an hour, with neither manuscript nor notes, she appeared as free as though giving an address was to her an everyday occurrence. Her voice was resonant, beautifully modulated. She gave to every word its proper value and to every thought the right inflection. Her manner of presentation was so natural, so unaffected, that the attention of her auditors remained wholly on the message and not at all upon the messenger who gave it.

The words she chose were as simple and direct as was the manner of her delivery. Although she never hesitated to make use of an apt illustration or a pertinent story to point a moral or to enhance the effectiveness of her message, there was no flowery rhetoric.

It is regrettable that there is no adequate report of this inspiring discourse. A stenographer was engaged to take the address, but his effort was a failure. Mrs. Eddy opened her message with the deeply impressive declaration that the ninety-first Psalm contains "more of meaning than is condensed into so many words anywhere else in all literature, except in the Sermon on the Mount." In this last sermon, giving the spiritual interpretation of the ninety-first Psalm, she testified to her love for and profound understanding of the Scriptures.

The soloist on this occasion had lost her voice eight years previously and had been fully restored to health by Christian Science. She sang Mrs. Eddy's "Communion Hymn" so beautifully that many of those present, knowing the story of her healing, were deeply touched.

A little over a year after she had spoken in Christian Science Hall, Mrs. Eddy addressed her followers again in Tremont Temple, Boston, on the occasion of the Annual Meeting of The Mother Church, in June, 1899. I remember this so well, as my sister Mary and I accompanied her. The previous year having witnessed a marked advance in all the activities of the church, the enemies of the Cause were active from rostrum and press in their attacks upon the movement and its Leader. It was declared by some of the more bitter element that Mrs. Eddy was a paralytic and unable to leave her room. But her visit to Boston at this Communion season, her appearance before her church in a public address of exhortation and inspiration, completely refuted these falsities.

On this memorable occasion, in June, 1899, so many students had come to Boston that in order to accommodate them it was necessary to hold four Communion services in the original Mother Church on Sunday, and it was estimated that nearly six thousand persons attended. Although Mrs. Eddy did not personally appear at these Sunday services, she sent a carefully prepared message which lifted her hearers above the realm of material sense to a spiritual apprehension of the great truths of being. She did, however, appear at the Annual Meeting, which was held the following Tuesday, having made the journey from Pleasant View on Monday especially for this purpose. A committee, delegated to meet Mrs. Eddy at the station in Boston, accompanied her to her former home at 385 Commonwealth Avenue, which was occupied by the First Reader of The Mother Church. Here she spent the night and remained until the hour of the Annual Meeting approached.

At two o'clock she left the First Reader's residence for Tremont Temple, which had been secured to accommodate the thousands who wished to attend the Annual Meeting. Going to the side entrance to avoid the throng, she found that the elevator was not running, and was forced to climb the long narrow stairway to the stage entrance. Here there was another flight of stairs to the platform from which she was to speak. This long climb she accomplished without fatigue.

As Judge Hanna conducted her to her place on the platform, the entire audience arose and remained standing in respectful silence until she was seated. After a brief introduction, Mrs. Eddy stood up before the great company of her devoted followers. Many were present who recalled her former appearance in the old Tremont Temple fourteen years earlier. Those of her students who remembered those days could not help noticing the contrast. Mrs. Eddy's name was now known and honored throughout the world. The churches established through her revelation circled the globe. At that former meeting she faced a hostile audience; now all seats were filled by her devoted followers. Formerly she met with derision and contempt; now she was received with honor and respect. Why? Because her words had been proved true by the multitudes. As she looked out upon the vast gathering of receptive listeners, each of whom had been blessed by her message, as she saw and felt the love which welled up from each heart, no wonder tears of joy dimmed her eyes.

I recall how calm and beautiful Mrs. Eddy appeared, simply attired in a gown of gray satin, covered with exquisite black lace. *The Boston Globe* reported:

> She looked as she sat there the ideal of the gentle, kindly old lady, who had led an uneventful life, and who was enjoying the peace and quiet of a conscience-clear old age. The lines on her face were soft, and there was nothing about her in repose to indicate the force of character and genius which she is credited with possessing.

Though brief, her address was inspiring and uplifting, for she spoke from deep experience when she said, "The Christian Scientist knows that spiritual faith and understanding pass through the waters of Meribah here—bitter waters; but he also knows they embark for infinity and anchor in omnipotence."[1] There were tears of joy in many eyes as she concluded with the words: "So shall all earth's children at last come to acknowledge God, and be one; inhabit His holy hill, the God-crowned summit of divine Science; the church militant rise to the church triumphant, and Zion be glorified."[2]

[1] The full text of this address now appears in Miscellany, pages 131–133.
[2] Miscellany, p. 133.

After delivering her address in Tremont Temple, Mrs. Eddy occupied a suite at the Parker House and there she received The Christian Science Board of Directors of The Mother Church and a few other friends. It was a happy company of grateful Scientists who gathered about their Leader. They saw her strong and free, untouched by the day's labor, and happy in the loyal and cordial reception everywhere accorded her by those eager to hear the message she had come to deliver.

The return journey to Concord was made without incident. A lunch had been provided for Mrs. Eddy, which she shared with all her company. She was especially pleased with a grape jelly layer cake, grape jelly being a favorite with her. Upon her arrival in Concord, Mrs. Eddy showed no signs of fatigue from her arduous labors and her busy hours in Boston. In her heart was a quiet joy and a thankful spirit that God had so lovingly smiled upon her efforts.

"Prayer first, preaching follows," Mrs. Eddy wrote at one time. The power of her sermons and public addresses lay in her own realization and patient demonstration of the truth she gave forth. Because she had been called upon to "pass through the waters of Meribah here—bitter waters," and had begun to "anchor in omnipotence," her very life was a sermon that healed and blessed friend and foe alike. She declared the only power her traducers possessed was to drive her nearer to God, and to compel her the more closely to wrap about her the mantle of divine Love.

Mrs. Eddy never sought personal recognition. It was her constant endeavor to instill in the consciousness of her followers the truth that it is God, divine Mind, who directs and leads the Cause of Christian Science. When The Christian Science Board of Directors, upon the completion of the original edifice of The Mother Church, presented it to their Leader and invited her to become its permanent pastor, she responded:

. . . If it will comfort you in the least, make me your *Pastor Emeritus,* nominally. Through my book, your textbook, I already speak to you each Sunday. You ask too much when asking me to accept your grand church edifice. . . .[1]

Thereafter Mary Baker Eddy was known as Pastor Emeritus of the Christian Science church. "Pastor Emeritus" in the old church meant one who had retired from active service but upon whom was bestowed an honorary title. When one contemplates the services rendered to The Mother Church from 1895 to 1910 by the Pastor Emeritus, however, it is evident that the term in this case did not symbolize retirement. Indeed, the world will some day realize that in modern history perhaps no one has achieved such eminent service for humanity's welfare as did Mary Baker Eddy from 1895 to 1910. The continuing use of this term on the title page of Science and Health indicates that it is the truth she uttered in her writings and practiced in her life that is today the Pastor Emeritus, the impersonal Pastor, Leader, and Teacher which Mrs. Eddy always strove to manifest while she was with us.

[1] "Pulpit and Press," p. 87.

Although it had served a definite purpose in the pioneer days of the movement, Mary Baker Eddy liberated her church from personal preaching when, in the year 1895, she gave to the Cause the following By-Law:

I, Mary Baker Eddy, ordain the BIBLE, and SCIENCE AND HEALTH WITH KEY TO THE SCRIPTURES, Pastor over The Mother Church, —The First Church of Christ, Scientist, in Boston, Mass.,—and they will continue to preach for this Church and the world.[1]

But could this startling innovation, ordaining the Bible and "Science and Health with Key to the Scriptures" as the impersonal pastor, prove a success? Could a church replace an eloquent preacher with two readers and still continue to grow and prosper? These questions disturbed many, including myself, who having but recently left the ranks of the clergy was accustomed to a personal preacher. But they did not disturb the Founder of the Christian Science movement. She asked only: What is God's direction? And as true as the needle to the pole, so true was she to the divine voice.

"The word of God, not human views, should preach to humanity," Mrs. Eddy once said to me. Ever seeking to meet the need of her church more perfectly, she had in mind a still further step in the ordination of the impersonal pastor, a step destined to bring greater blessing to mankind. It was an education to observe this great woman as she obediently followed the leading of divine Mind in the spiritual evolution of the divine plan.

This further step in the unfoldment of the impersonal pastor was the gift to the world of the Christian Science

[1] Church Manual, Art. XIV, Sect. 1.

Bible Lessons as they now regularly appear in the *Christian Science Quarterly;* however, the publication of the Christian Science Bible Lessons in their first form began in January, 1890. Then the lessons were from the "International Series" and were commented on by parallel references from the Bible and correlative selections from "Science and Health with Key to the Scriptures." This was the form of the lesson when the Bible and Science and Health first became pastor, and was read by two readers in lieu of a sermon.

A further step was taken by Mrs. Eddy when three years later, in 1898, she instructed the Bible Lesson Committee to prepare lessons from a series of twenty-six subjects which she gave them. From July of that year these Lesson-Sermons appeared in the *Christian Science Quarterly* and were read at the first service, and the lesson from the "International Series" was read at the second service, if such was held. In less than a year from that time the use of the "International Series" was discontinued, and from then on, wherever two services are held, the Lesson-Sermon for the day is repeated.

The founding of the *Quarterly* proved to be a glorious gift to the Christian Science movement. It was a signal instance of Mrs. Eddy's inspired wisdom in uniting the entire Christian Science movement in one method of Bible study, one basis of teaching in the Sunday school, and one form of preaching in all Christian Science churches throughout the world. For not only do the Bible Lessons form the Sunday sermons, but through their daily study they provide the chief part of the spiritual food so essential to the health, well-being, and growth of every Christian Science student.

Some years after the establishment of these Bible Lessons a member of the committee expressed dissatisfaction that the subjects which Mrs. Eddy had provided for the Bible Lessons numbered only twenty-six. A committee of workers in The Mother Church, feeling that there ought at least to be one subject for every Sunday in the year, proceeded to compile an additional list of twenty-six subjects. As a member of the Bible Lesson Committee, with my home in Concord, I was requested to present them to Mrs. Eddy.

Not until many weeks after doing so did I hear anything further with regard to these proposed subjects. In company with others, on September 13, 1901, I was called to Pleasant View on a matter of business for Mrs. Eddy, and the little company was gathered in conference in the library. When the business was finished, Mrs. Eddy called me to a seat beside her and, turning to me, she said, so energetically that I almost jumped from the sofa, "That will never do—that will never do!" What she meant I did not know, but not leaving me long in ignorance, she continued: "The additional list of topics sent me for the Lessons are needless. They can all be used under the present list of subjects, which include every one of those you gave me. Tell the committee the original subjects were given of God—they are sufficient, and they will remain forever."

This message still rings in my ears. Mrs. Eddy's bearing, the flash in her eye, the tone of her voice, as she uttered the words, have etched themselves upon my memory. This historical incident was characteristic of Mrs. Eddy's conduct of her Cause. When convinced that she was acting in obedience to Principle, no amount of contrary influence could swerve her one hair's breadth from the line of God's appointing.

CHAPTER X

ALMOST immediately after founding the Christian Science church, Mrs. Eddy perceived the necessity of safeguarding the movement and its Founder by making definite provision for correcting innocent misunderstandings, erroneous statements, and malicious attacks that appeared in the public press.

For this purpose Mrs. Eddy eventually established the Committee on Publication, but in the very early days of Christian Science she herself carried on the work and replied to critics of Christian Science in a direct, convincing, and usually brief manner. No matter how bitter or untrue the attack, Mrs. Eddy's reply was always reasonable, moderate, and free from resentment. She always appealed to the thought and not to the prejudices of her readers. In the early days when Christian Science was not so generally accepted as it is today, Mrs. Eddy's rare skill in meeting the attacks of critics not only convinced them of their mistakes but often turned them into friends and supporters.

Acting as her own committee, or through the Publication Committees, Mrs. Eddy made use of the press in behalf of the Cause in innumerable ways. Thus, cases of healing sent to her by letter were published; Wednesday evening testimony meetings reported; her annual messages to The Mother Church printed; lectures inserted in local papers; false charges against Christian

Science practice answered; and misrepresentation by critics corrected. In this way, publicity was given to the building of The Mother Church and of the church in Concord; favorable articles about Christian Science or its followers reprinted; false charges concerning her church repudiated; misstatements about her textbook corrected; historical facts regarding her life given out; reports of annual meetings and of special services of The Mother Church and of the Concord church reported; publicity given to Christian Science prison work. Gifts to the church were reported; her views on subjects uppermost in public thought stated; visits of Christian Scientists to Concord were reported; interviews given to newspaper reporters; comments made on helpful state legislation; news reports of dedication services of branch churches reprinted, and public tribute paid to those laboring to serve humanity. Many other items of importance to the Cause and its Leader were also published.

During many active years, Mrs. Eddy used every legitimate occasion to bring Christian Science before the public, and always with good results. Her success was in no small measure due to the fact that, as she once said to her household, "I have found that the *when* is as important as the *how*."

When undergoing persecution and trial, there were brief periods in which non-Scientists rose up and championed her Cause. Here and there were welcome signs to comfort and encourage the hard-pressed Founder of Christian Science. Among those who thus spoke in her behalf was a clergyman, the Rev. Frank L. Phalen, one-time resident of Concord, New Hampshire, and pastor of the Unitarian Church. When the Rev. Mr. Phalen moved to Fairhaven, Massachusetts, the *Fairhaven Star* printed a sermon which he preached there on "Liberty," in which he said in part:

In the act of denying liberty to our friends in the Christian Science church we deny liberty to ourselves, liberty to everybody. The assailants of Christian Science reveal their own ignorance, their own wicked hearts, their absolute denial of Jesus Christ.

I know Mrs. Eddy, and I do not know one single fact against her. . . .

I have never met, or seen, or heard of anybody who could prove in a court of law anything against her purity, her honesty, her spirituality.

. . . She practices what she preaches. This confirms my opinion that Mrs. Eddy, to speak very moderately and with a careful conservatism, is a remarkable woman. She is the most remarkable woman I know anything about in Europe or America at this moment.

Prior to the establishment of the Committee on Publication as it is now constituted, Mrs. Eddy had made a By-Law which provided for a committee of three to deal with the press under her supervision. Proceeding carefully to evolve the instrument best fitted to meet the demands of the situation, she gave instructions that the newly formed Committee for The Mother Church of Boston, Massachusetts, should be thoroughly prepared to reply to any statement regarding Christian Science appearing in the press. The first Committee on Publication was originally known as the Publishing Committee.

Shortly after taking up my residence in Concord, I was appointed by Mrs. Eddy to serve, under her guidance, as Committee on Publication for the State of New Hampshire. I soon found there was much to be done in replying to unfavorable criticism from hostile critics, but nothing daunted Mrs. Eddy. Attacks on her, however, gradually abated, and during the later years very little appeared in the local press unfavorable to Christian Science or its Leader. While many clergymen occupied the pulpits of the Concord churches during the last nine years of Mrs. Eddy's residence there, only three sermons were preached against Christian Science. On a few occasions, indeed, some misguided persons attempted to assail Mrs. Eddy's teachings and to belittle her character, but these attempts only ended in failure and in raising up friends in her behalf. She herself declared that temporary opposition was but the prophecy of future success.

Mrs. Eddy's moves were always a source of interest to the press, who seized upon every opportunity to give publicity, sometimes favorable, and sometimes unfavorable, to the words and acts of the Founder of Christian Science. She always did her best to co-operate with the press in every way possible. When the *New York Journal,* at the time of the Annual Meeting in June, 1901, requested a photograph and an account of the visit of Christian Scientists to see Mrs. Eddy at Pleasant View, she asked me to prepare a suitable article and to forward the desired photographs.

Mrs. Eddy took great care to curb even the well-meaning efforts of kindly critics in her behalf, and in May, 1900, requested *The Boston Herald* to publish the following statement:

I even hope that those who are kind enough to speak well of me may do so honestly and not too earnestly, and this seldom, until mankind learn more of my meaning and can speak justly of my living.[1]

"I find it more troublesome to be overrated publicly than underrated," she wrote to the *Concord Evening Monitor,* "since conscience requires a bit of my time to correct the former, while happily the latter old time will correct." After an interview with Mrs. Eddy a newspaper printed the following:

Some time since, . . . an eminent lawyer wrote a booklet . . . in which he sharply criticizes those offering unjust and unmerited attacks from the pulpit upon Christian Science and its founder, Rev. Mary Baker G. Eddy.

A representative of the press called on Mrs. Eddy to ascertain her views . . . and to the newspaper man she said:

"Upon reading the grand preface of [the] book, I laid it aside from lack of time just then, and sent my compliments to the author with an order for said book. After perusing his book thoroughly, I changed my opinion, not of the author's talents, scholarship, and high intent (although I have never seen him), but of the advisability of publishing the book, and immediately requested the parties to discontinue publishing it in its present form of treating the subject. I did this, solely, because the author's vehemence in denouncing the pulpit's furious attacks upon me was not consonant with my Christian sentiment. It is written of our great Master whose life and teachings furnish my model that 'When he was reviled he reviled not again.' "

Encouraging evidences of a more enlightened and intelligent attitude on the part of the public were occasionally brought to Mrs. Eddy's attention by the Committee on Publication. In December, 1904, in the course

[1] Miscellany, p. 264.

of a conversation at Pleasant View, she spoke of a certain prominent person who had taken a strong stand for ideal philosophy. "He has shown the inadequacy of material philosophy," she remarked, "and has taken his stand for the spiritual interpretation of the universe." These progressive signs of the leavening activity of Truth she welcomed with keen joy.

Mrs. Eddy was most exact in instructing the members of the Publication Committee regarding their dealings with the press. At one time she sent me the following precise directions:

> . . . You are to go to Boston with these articles and if Mr. Farlow[1] is not in Boston to attend to it, *you* are to stay and have it put into the paper so it will come out in the Herald tomorrow morning without fail. It *must* be done and you must see that it is done word for word correctly. This is *most important*.

Mrs. Eddy expected her workers to exercise intelligence in carrying out her instructions, however, and not to act as mere puppets. Before arranging to have her Message to The Mother Church for 1900 published in the periodicals, Mrs. Eddy sent me the manuscript with no instructions other than to have it printed in booklet form, that she might have it available for distribution. Taking the manuscript to a local printer, I watched the proofs and took the completed work to Mrs. Eddy. With the exception of one important item, she was pleased with the pamphlet. The Message having come to me without a title, I had allowed it to be printed thus, and Mrs. Eddy justly complained that I and others had neglected our

[1] At that time Alfred Farlow was serving as Committee on Publication for The Mother Church.

duty in not calling this point to her consideration. At this time, not being a seasoned Christian Scientist, I was like the printer's devil who was told to follow copy even if it took him out of the window, and so had felt it necessary to follow Mrs. Eddy's copy slavishly.

In the Concord *People and Patriot* of August 13, 1900, appeared an interview with Mrs. Eddy which disclosed a subtle attempt to injure her and the Cause which she so ably defended:

The following from a Boston paper of Saturday is of interest to the Concord public:

"For a number of months reports have been sent out from Concord, the home of Mrs. Mary Baker Eddy, founder of the Christian Science faith, to the effect that Mrs. Eddy is suffering from cancer and has not long to live.

"Recently a story was sent from Concord to the effect that Mrs. Eddy was under the care of a doctor of medicine. This report tended to show that Mrs. Eddy had abandoned the Christian Science principle of healing. . . . It has stirred Mrs. Eddy to make a vigorous denial of it, and also of the statement that she is sick, which she does in an interview, the essential points of which are as follows:

" 'I am well despite the many attempts of those opposed to the principles of Christian Science to prove otherwise. For 34 years I have labored in this great field and never have I been so keenly alive to the glorious privilege of living and working.

" 'You have asked me if it were true that I am a sufferer with cancer. You have asked me if it is true that a doctor of medicine is in attendance upon me.

" 'To both these questions I answer no with all the truth in my being. I am free from disease and there is but one physician guarding my welfare. He is the great physician.

" 'Stories telling of my illness have been, I am sorry to say, industriously circulated. They are naught but malicious falsehoods. Their object, I presume, is to discredit the belief and

[153]

practice of the [one] in the principles she has expounded for more than thirty years. This, indeed, would be much to those who are opposed to the growth of the science of Christ.

"'For many years I have been aware of what you tell me, and in a quiet way I have battled against these unseen enemies of the faith.

"'With your own eyes you can see that I am well and strong, although the circle of years usually allotted to man has passed over my head.' . . .

"The interviewer describes Mrs. Eddy as 'singularly graceful and winning in her bearing. Her figure is tall, slender and flexible in movement as a Delsarte disciple. Her face is oval in shape, the features regular, yet indicative of strong character. Her eyes are a luminous blue, a bright contrast to the mass of wavy white hair that falls over her temples.

"'Mrs. Eddy is a striking picture of health in old age. Her step is firm, and she walks with an easy grace, and strongly conveys the impression of health and strength.'"

In the year 1907, after years of service to humanity, which expressed itself in numberless ways, Mrs. Eddy found herself the victim of a modern form of religious persecution superlatively cruel and vindictive because of the subtle and hidden nature of its venomous intent. A malicious legal attack disguising itself under the name of friendship began when a New York newspaper, thinking it could increase its circulation, instigated a campaign of slander against the revered Leader of Christian Science. The newspaper, combined with certain foes of Mrs. Eddy in New Hampshire, persuaded her son to join them in what purported to be an effort to protect his aged mother from the faithful followers who were nearest to her. This despicable attack, known as the "Next Friends Suit," was an attempted exploitation, not

Leaving Pleasant View for her daily drive, 1900

only of the Discoverer and Founder of Christian Science, but of the religion which she had founded.

After almost a year of continuous, unjust prosecution, the withdrawal of the suit came suddenly following a visit paid to Mrs. Eddy at Pleasant View by the masters' court, and counsel for both defendants and plaintiffs. She had exhibited such mental alertness during this ordeal that it was plainly evident that she was eminently capable of administering her own affairs.

The outcome of this suit was a complete vindication of Mrs. Eddy and of the Cause for which she had labored for nearly half a century. Once again, her able wielding of "the sword of the Spirit" had triumphed over the prince of darkness. In the face of worldly hate, she beheld the prophecy of Isaiah (54:17) gloriously fulfilled:

No weapon that is formed against thee shall prosper; and every tongue that shall rise against thee in judgment thou shalt condemn.

The deep waters through which she journeyed during this experience were indicated by words she voiced to me shortly after the close of the trial. It was the implied threat to the Cause of Christian Science, the Cause she loved and for which she had labored and sacrificed, that pierced her heart. She said, as I vividly recall her words:

I don't care what mortal sense has done; I don't care how it has insulted me, wronged me, and lied about me. It is all past and it is a dream. I have found Love at last. I can lie down in the Father's arms and be at peace. I love God supremely; mortal sense has done its worst; I have passed through the Red Sea, and under the rod, and still I am God's own child, hid with Christ in His arms, safe in His green pastures.

CHAPTER XI

MRS. EDDY writes on page 58 of Science and Health: "Home is the dearest spot on earth, and it should be the centre, though not the boundary, of the affections."

These words are highly significant, for throughout her whole life the idea conveyed by the word "home" had a special meaning for Mrs. Eddy, and no matter whether she was temporarily occupying a single room, living in a rented apartment, or dwelling in her own house, she possessed the happy faculty of investing her surroundings with a true sense of home.

On one occasion, as I recall, Mrs. Eddy said to the members of her household: "Home is not a place but a power. We find home when we arrive at the full understanding of God. Home! Think of it! Where sense has no claims and Soul satisfies."

Mrs. Eddy's home at Pleasant View was a splendid example of her vision and foresight, for she literally transformed what had once been ugly and desolate into a home of beauty, comfort, and peace. When she was living on State Street in Concord, New Hampshire, the noise frequently disturbed her work and very naturally made her wish for a quiet home in the country. On her drives her attention had often been drawn to a site occupied by a group of unsightly buildings very much in need of repair. One day as Mrs. Eddy was passing the place

Pleasant View

"her peaceful home, where she dwelt for sixteen eventful . . . years"

the clouds suddenly parted and the sun shone down on it, illuminating it like a spotlight. She glimpsed the vision of its transformation and promptly arranged to purchase the tract of land. It was not long before she had improved the grounds, erected stables, rebuilt and added to the main dwelling, making it almost unrecognizable from its former dilapidated condition. (This is the beautiful spot upon which is now located "The Pleasant View Home.")

"A home should be something more than four walls," Mrs. Eddy said to me. "There should be about it noble trees, beautiful shrubbery, flowers, vines clambering over the house, and a rose garden." And that is what she made of the desolate spot transformed into Pleasant View, her peaceful home, where she dwelt for sixteen eventful but happy years.

At her Pleasant View home, there was beauty everywhere. Around the porches of the house clambered vines in which the birds nested. On the front lawn there was a summerhouse surrounded by a beautiful bed of pansies. A flower-bordered walk led to the little pond, a loving gift from a group of grateful Christian Scientists. Mrs. Eddy was very fond of roses and her rose garden was a delight to all. Particularly fond also of pink flowers, she was delighted over a Paul's double-flowering thorn, planted within sight of her study window. She also dearly loved the Mayflower, the trailing arbutus, which as a child she had gathered near her home at Bow. She was very fond, too, of the Japanese quince, which blooms early in the spring. "I love the symbol of the morning glory," she said at one time, "with its bright promise of the coming of the light." Mrs. Eddy had always loved flowers, and when she first came to Concord she was so often seen with flowers that the children came to call her "the flower lady."

Mrs. Eddy truly enjoyed her home. "The strongest tie I have ever felt," said Mrs. Eddy one evening, after we had been singing hymns, "next to my love of God, has been my love for home." One of her students told me of her first visit to Mrs. Eddy shortly after the establishment of the Commonwealth Avenue residence in Boston. Mrs. Eddy showed her caller over the entire house from cellar to attic, from the kitchen and pantry to the bedrooms. The hostess pointed out the wardrobes; nothing escaped her eye, nothing was unworthy of mention. After they had viewed the entire house, as they were coming down the front stairs, Mrs. Eddy put her arm around the student and said tenderly, "I want every one of my students to have homes of their own."

Mrs. Eddy was a deep lover of beauty. She held beauty as symbolizing the purity, the loveliness of Soul. Beauty, she felt, was a quality of divine Mind which finds expression in one's environment, in one's appearance, and in every other detail of daily life. She instinctively appreciated the beautiful in art.

Mrs. Eddy displayed excellent taste in the selection of her wardrobe. Having little or no time for shopping, she was grateful to allow one or two of her students who understood her needs and tastes, to purchase gowns, bonnets, gloves, and accessories for her in Boston or

New York. About her bonnets she was very particular. They had to be just right. In the latter part of 1907, she was fortunate in securing an experienced dressmaker, a student of Christian Science, who came to the house. Mrs. Eddy regarded the making of a dress as a great achievement. She had a fondness for certain colors: her gowns, coats, hats, and accessories were for the most part soft shades of purple, lavender, and pink,[1] or old rose— although she frequently chose gray or white. When attired for the street, she invariably wore white kid gloves. Mrs. Eddy walked very quickly and gracefully. I remember seeing her one afternoon, beautifully dressed, wearing the diamond cross given her by a student and the exquisite breastpin presented to her by the Daughters of the American Revolution. She looked regal, a picture of harmony and refinement.

Mrs. Eddy was always pleased to see her followers well-dressed. As an instance of this, one of her students received word to go to Pleasant View one day, just as she was about to make an afternoon call. She was wearing a new gown for the occasion, and although she was rather reluctant to appear before her Leader so fashionably dressed, there was no time to change before catching her train. She planned to offer profuse apologies, but before she could say a word Mrs. Eddy exclaimed, "Oh, what a beautiful gown! I love to see my students well-dressed."

[1] Her liking for pink and rose found expression in the double parlors at Pleasant View and Chestnut Hill, attractively decorated in these colors. The upstairs living room at Chestnut Hill, where the family gathered for morning song service, was named the "pink room."

Although Mrs. Eddy had a number of photographs taken and a few portraits were painted from some of her photographs, none of these did her justice. She did not feel that she could spare the time for photographers. She did, nevertheless, tell the well-known Concord photographer, her friend, Mr. W. G. C. Kimball, that he might take her picture if he could do so without inconveniencing her. His opportunity occurred in 1903, when the Christian Scientists in attendance at the Annual Meeting of The Mother Church paid a visit to Pleasant View, by Mrs. Eddy's invitation. At this time he took the well-known and popular photograph called the "Balcony Portrait." However, he was at such a distance from the balcony that he felt the photograph was of no real value and he threw the original among his discards.

Sometime later, in cleaning up his studio he found the balcony photograph and was about to throw it away. On second thought he decided to enlarge it, and lo, the famous "Balcony Portrait" was the outcome!

Many years later, when my wife and I paid a visit to Mr. Kimball's studio, in speaking of the incident he said, with a twinkle in his eye, "It was lucky I didn't throw it away, for that 'Balcony Portrait' has brought me more business than all the others put together."

Mrs. Eddy liked people to be natural, simple, and unaffected. She quickly detected anything that was false, pretentious, or artificial, and instantly appraised an individual at his true value. She once said in effect to me, "My first estimate of a man, formed sometimes without seeing him, always turns out to be right."

Addressing her followers, 1903

Often Mrs. Eddy entertained the members of her household at Pleasant View or Chestnut Hill with amusing tales of her childhood or sprightly comments on current events. She was not only fond of telling a good story herself, but delighted in listening to the wit and humor of others. At the dinner table at Pleasant View one day a clergyman remarked that Scripture had occasionally been used by preachers in two ways: one in which the sermon was unfolded from the text; the other, where the Scripture was but a pretext. "That is true," said Mrs. Eddy. "I always liked the Bible sermon which grew naturally from the Word. A wit once said of a certain preacher's sermons that if the text had the smallpox, the sermon never would catch it! Such sermons remind me of the close-fisted old farmer who at the table was stingy with the food, but in the field greedy to get much work from the help. At the table, then, he solemnly quoted the Scripture, 'Let your moderation be known unto all men,' but in the hayfield, 'Whatsoever thy hand findeth to do, do it with thy might.' Not less unfair," she continued, "are those critics who tear apart passages in Science and Health from their proper import and twist them to their own false meaning."

At this point she was reminded of a young clergyman who had for the first time preached a sermon before his senior pastor and who was insistent that his elder pass an opinion upon it. "Well," ventured the old parson, "there was one passage that especially pleased me." "What passage was that?" eagerly asked the younger. "It was the passage from the pulpit to the vestry," was the response.

But more frequently a deeper note crept into her conversations, as Mrs. Eddy brought out some underlying metaphysical point or paused to give a word of counsel and admonition. "A landlord once had a poor tenant whom he wanted to get rid of," she once told us, "but the tenant liked the house too well to leave. At length, the owner took off the chimney; then he took out the windows; until at last the tenant was willing to take himself out! Thus it is with us," she continued, "we want to get rid only of the pains of material sense, but we do not wish to part with its pleasures, which are equally false. But we will be willing to part with the flesh when we find no joy in the flesh."

In addition to her appreciation of good literature, Mrs. Eddy had always been a lover of music. When she was living on State Street in Concord she sang soprano in a little home quartet. At Chestnut Hill, after the early morning duties were cared for, members of her household would be invited into the "pink room" for a service of song. Mrs. Eddy loved the familiar gospel hymns, and I well remember the sweet quality of her voice. She enjoyed listening to a member of the household who sang a high soprano. Also at Chestnut Hill there was a piano player and a Victrola, and although Mrs. Eddy seldom listened to the piano player she took keen pleasure in a few of the recordings by leading musicians for the Victrola.

An outstanding characteristic of Mrs. Eddy's home life was her unceasing thoughtfulness and consideration for others. With her, it was literally true that "to live was to love." In spite of her prodigious labors in behalf of a world-encircling movement, Mrs. Eddy, nevertheless, found time for bestowing those little personal attentions on others that give such sweet savor to human existence. She was constantly remembering, with little acts of kindness, the members of her household and those of her followers who lived near her, sharing with them flowers, fruit, and candy. Mrs. Eddy's love in the home was always such a gloriously spontaneous expression. For example, I recall, on a certain occasion, when admiring a lovely bouquet of long-stemmed roses that stood upon her table, she said, "You do love the flowers, don't you? And a flower is a symbol of infinite good." Later in the day I found the bouquet in my room with a note asking me to "Please accept the flowers *and the vase*." This vase is still in my possession and is a reminder of Mrs. Eddy's thoughtfulness in little things, of a love that looked upon her possessions as not for self alone, but to be shared graciously with others. When a beautiful night-blooming cereus was about to flower at Pleasant View, a secretary sent an invitation to one of her students and his friends to view it: "If you are fond of flowers and would like to see something nice, take a walk out to Pleasant View this evening, at nine o'clock or after, but not before."

On one occasion Mrs. Eddy presented a pair of gloves to a faithful helper. The gift prompted this letter of thanks from him:

Dear Mrs. Eddy: . . . It seems hard to find words to express my gratitude, for I owe so much to you, so much, in fact, that I fear I shall never be able to pay it.

When Science and Health came to me, I had nothing in this

world but husks, and they were almost gone. God has indeed been kind to me, in that I have been permitted to come to Pleasant View to do what I can do. And when I see how kindly you appreciate even the little that I may be able to do, it almost melts my heart within me, and it is this thought that I prize infinitely higher than the gift itself.

Thanking you kindly, I wish you a happy New Year. May God bless you.

In 1903, the Executive Members of The Mother Church presented Mrs. Eddy with a loving cup as a token of their tender regard. Among the numerous expressions of gratitude that poured in from near and far was a beautiful copy of the Martin Luther Bible, printed in 1733. Presented by friends in Hannover, Germany, the Bible, bound in leather over oaken boards, with silver trimmings, bore engraved upon its clasp Mrs. Eddy's name. Of this rare gift, with which our Leader was much pleased, the *Concord Daily Monitor* reported:

UNIQUE GIFT FROM GERMANY.

Concord has recently had two visitors who came here upon an unusual and unique errand. These visitors . . . crossed the water to pay their respects to an eminent citizen of Concord, Mary Baker Eddy, and to present her with a beautiful and valuable copy of the German Bible, the gift of the Christian Scientists of Germany.

But when Christian Scientists from all over the world began to deluge Mrs. Eddy with gifts, she found it necessary to restrain their well-intentioned generosity for fear that too much attention be paid to her personality and too little time be left for things of the Spirit. "I want no material gifts," Mrs. Eddy said in substance at this time,

"I want spiritual gifts. I would rather have demonstrations made by my students in healing the sick, than to have all the gifts on earth. These are the gifts I want: your own spiritual growth, your own demonstrations."

Although none of the members of Mrs. Eddy's immediate family accepted Christian Science, some of her relatives expressed a friendly feeling toward the Discoverer and Founder of Christian Science. One of these was her cousin, General Henry M. Baker. He served in the New Hampshire Senate and was later elected to Congress. General Baker always cherished an affection toward his cousin, and in 1907 he was appointed by Mrs. Eddy to serve as one of the trustees of her property.

One could not be long in the presence of that great woman without realizing the remarkable efficiency with which she managed her affairs. Her daily program, three hundred and sixty-five days in the year, with which nothing was permitted to interfere, I well remember. Because of the regularity of her life and the orderly manner in which she conducted her activities, she was able to accomplish what the ordinary worker would consider impossible. Mrs. Eddy was always a "minute woman." She said that Christian Scientists, having Principle as their measuring rod, should be the most methodical people in the world in the ordering of their personal lives, their homes, and their business affairs.

Except for her daily drive, an occasional interchange of conversation, or now and then a little interlude of singing with the members of her household gathered about the piano, Mrs. Eddy had no recreation. At Pleasant View she arose at six, breakfasted at seven, dined at twelve, and had supper at six. The early morning hours, until nine o'clock, she devoted to prayer and meditation. Then her letters were brought to her, and the early part of the forenoon was devoted to her correspondence. From her childhood, Mrs. Eddy had written her letters in her lap, but as her correspondence increased in volume, she dictated some of her replies. In the early days, Calvin Frye examined the incoming mail and turned the important letters over to Mrs. Eddy. But as the years passed and her labors for the Cause increased, she had less and less time to give to details, so that most of the routine correspondence was attended to by one or another of her secretaries. I recall at one time that she kept five secretaries busy.

In addition to her correspondence, her literary work occupied a great amount of time and demanded devoted attention. During these busy years she was always writing something for the Cause, in one form or another: articles, messages to The Mother Church, to the Concord church, to other branch churches near and far, letters of counsel and admonition to students in distant fields, contributions to the newspapers and magazines.

The dinner hour was twelve o'clock noon, and everyone was expected to be promptly on hand. Although for many years Mrs. Eddy dined with the members of her household, in the latter years of her life she preferred the privacy of her study, where she might continue uninterrupted whatever she might be engaged in at the time. The bill of fare included such foods as suited the tastes of the household, but neither tea nor coffee was served at either Pleasant View or Chestnut Hill. I can still recall the drumming sound of the old icecream freezer in the basement, busily preparing one of Mrs. Eddy's favorite daily dishes. I well remember that she did not countenance tardiness at meals. On one occasion a member of the family was so late in coming down to breakfast that she met Mrs. Eddy going up the stairway from the dining room. When she expressed surprise at this, Mrs. Eddy replied that breakfast was finished, and it certainly was for the late comer.

When I first knew Mrs. Eddy, she took her daily drive at two o'clock, riding out into the surrounding country and sometimes not returning until four. But as the Cause grew, and her labors and responsibilities became heavier, she went out in her carriage only from one to two, passing through the leading streets of Concord and the suburbs. Usually a woman companion accompanied her on her drive. Occasionally she would invite one of her students who might be visiting in Concord. After she moved to her Chestnut Hill residence she enjoyed driving through the boulevards and highways bordering upon her estate, and along the Chestnut Hill reservoir.

Mrs. Eddy did not care for the automobile. Although she owned cars for the use of the members of her household, only on one occasion did she ride in one of them. She much preferred her reliable pair of horses, Major and Princess, for she felt that she knew them and that they knew her.

On returning from her drive in the afternoon, Mrs.

Eddy saw her callers: officers of The Mother Church, her students, visiting Christian Scientists, or others with whom she had important conferences. This necessary business completed, she returned to her work.

Whenever possible, Mrs. Eddy did her best to finish the day's activities before the evening meal, but often the exacting nature of her work prevented this. Indeed, when occasion demanded it, she did not hesitate to work far into the night to accomplish something of importance to the welfare of her Cause. But when no such demands pressed in upon her, she permitted herself the privilege of a little leisure at the close of the day. From childhood she had loved to sit by the window at eventide and look out upon the stars and upon the lights of the town. Now in this later period, taking her seat in the comfortable rocker as the shadows fell, she watched the lights come on in the driveway. When this brief interlude ended, the rest of the evening was usually given to reading, study, and devotion, and often she invited to her study some members of the household for counsel and instruction.

It was the custom of the various members of the household to stop and say good-night to Mrs. Eddy after supper. On her desk was a little clock so arranged that a tiny light illumined its face, and when anyone entered the room where she sat working and praying, this little beam lighted up the darkness. One night a worker came in, pointed to the light and said, "While the light holds out to burn, the vilest sinner may return." Instantly Mrs. Eddy replied, "While the light is burning bright, the best of Christians comes in sight."

"the room where she sat working and praying"

In spite of the thousand and one demands on her time, Mrs. Eddy found opportunity to oversee the management of her home and thoroughly to train the workers whom she called there. The executive ability she so ably manifested in the conduct of the Christian Science movement, she applied with equal effectiveness to the running of her home. So smoothly adjusted was the domestic machinery of her household that the maximum of results was obtained with a minimum of labor.

At the opening of the century, Mrs. Eddy's household at Pleasant View was small, consisting only of a secretary or two, a companion, a cook, a housekeeper, and additional outside workers; but as the Cause grew and her work became more exacting, others were called to meet various needs of the household. In the early days, Mr. Calvin Frye faithfully undertook whatever duties and tasks required his attention: he kept her books, superintended the household buying, took her dictation, typing or writing in longhand a vast number of her letters and most of her articles. Mrs. Eddy's inspiration seemed to have no limits; for example, when she was teaching at her Massachusetts Metaphysical College in Boston, in the early morning hours before she met with the class, she was dictating to Mr. Frye that wonderful book, "Unity of Good."

Calvin Frye is entitled to the highest praise for his fidelity to the Cause of Christian Science, and for the vast amount of work which he willingly did for Mrs. Eddy. She enjoyed his wit and found him one who was ever ready to fulfill the many demands made upon him.

Calvin Frye was much interested in mechanical developments and was a steady subscriber to technical magazines. When it was announced that an airplane meet would take place at Squantum, Massachusetts, Mr. Frye and other members of the household very much wished to attend. Mrs. Eddy agreed that the household should be divided into two groups to go on separate days. Accordingly, on the first day, when Calvin Frye had finished his duties, he jumped into the White steamer automobile which was waiting at the door and was off to Squantum.

The little group returned to the family circle at five that afternoon. This was the longest vacation Mr. Frye had taken in all his twenty-eight years of service.

Although home was the "centre," it was certainly not the "boundary of the affections"[1] for Mary Baker Eddy. Despite the ceaseless demands of her Cause, Mrs. Eddy never failed to keep in touch with the important happenings of the day. During her stay in Concord, the two local dailies, the *People and Patriot* and the *Concord Evening Monitor*, as well as other timely publications, came regularly to her study. There was nothing provincial about Mrs. Eddy's outlook. She was, if ever anyone was, a woman of wide interests, concerned in the welfare of all nations and peoples. She was also an ideal hostess. Whether conversing in her study with a single student, or entertaining hundreds of her followers on the lawn at Pleasant View, she radiated a love that made her guests feel free from all restraint and

[1] Science and Health, p. 58.

at ease in her company. Mrs. Eddy was a rare conversationalist, and an hour spent in her company was a blessing never to be forgotten. She was interested primarily in the spiritual progress of her students, not in their personalities. And, incidentally, she discouraged any tendency of her followers to pay any undue attention to *her* personality. Apropos of this, she one day said to some of the members of her household at Chestnut Hill, as I later recorded:

> Look to divine Principle. A student once said to me, "I feel better if I can see you every day!" I replied, "If you feel that way, don't come to see me. Turn your thought entirely away from me. You will find me in my writings, not in the flesh."

A happy household was domiciled at Chestnut Hill, as these words of Mrs. Eddy make plain:

> The Christian Scientists at Mrs. Eddy's home are the happiest group on earth. Their faces shine with the reflection of light and love; their footsteps are not weary; their thoughts are upward; their way is onward, and their light shines. The world is better for this happy group of Christian Scientists; Mrs. Eddy is happier because of them; God is glorified in His reflection of peace, love, joy.[1]

An entire volume might be written about Mrs. Eddy's friendships. Not only a multitude of her own followers, but many who had no understanding of Christian Science, looked upon her with respect. Her affections went forth to all, and whoever responded to this love was her friend. This friendship was manifested not only in words of counsel and acts of love but in pointed, timely rebukes. Although occasionally they hurt at the moment, they

[1] Miscellany, p. 355.

proved to be a healing fire, destroying only the error. A member of the household once asked her, "Do you love me?" One should have seen Mrs. Eddy's face; she looked in wonderment at such a question. After a thoughtful pause, she replied, "I just love. As the sun just shines, I just love."

Among Mrs. Eddy's friends were a number of children, some of whom she met on her daily drives as her carriage passed along the outskirts of Concord. Eagerly watching for her coming, they readily responded to the love she radiated. She waved to them, threw kisses, and often distributed candies among her small friends. One little fellow in Concord, who cherished a warm feeling "for the lady in the carriage," had learned who she was and where she lived. Now, it happened that a gentleman acquainted with the boy's family came to Concord to visit them, and he was very anxious to meet Mrs. Eddy. Having tried to persuade several members of the household to present him, with no success, he had become discouraged. "I'll introduce you to Mrs. Eddy," said the boy. Concealing his doubts, the man readily accepted the little fellow's offer, and followed him to Pleasant View. Together they entered the grounds and there saw Mrs. Eddy standing on the balcony. When she called to ask her little friend what he wanted, he told her, and with characteristic kindness Mrs. Eddy invited him and his friend to come in to see her. The gentleman's experience reminded him of the Scripture, "and a little child shall lead them."

The first occasion on which I was privileged to be the

guest of Mary Baker Eddy was the fifth of July, 1897, the day celebrated as Independence Day, since the fourth fell on Sunday. I was one of a vast host who journeyed to Pleasant View in response to the following invitation read at the Communion service:

MY BELOVED CHURCH:—I invite you, one and all, to Pleasant View, Concord, N. H., on July 5, at 12:30 P. M., if you would enjoy so long a trip for so small a purpose as simply seeing Mother.[1]

On that memorable day the beloved Leader of a great religious movement welcomed and addressed two thousand five hundred of her followers from all parts of the United States and from other countries, on the lawn of her beautiful estate. At the railroad station her followers were given a cordial welcome by the townspeople of Concord. Guests were invited from Concord, including Mayor Woodworth, who heartily welcomed the company with a friendly address.

On the lawn, awaiting the coming of Mrs. Eddy, hundreds of people had gathered. She soon appeared and took her seat in a haircloth armchair upon the veranda. So calm, so still was she that her presence seemed to breathe forth benediction on those present. When she rose to give her address, her voice was so clear, her enunciation so distinct, that no one had the least difficulty in hearing every word she said. Never before had I seen a speaker arrest and hold the attention of an audience as did Mary Baker Eddy.

In her face and manner appeared no thought of self, but a deep concern and love for the mighty Cause she

[1] Miscellany, p. 169.

[173]

served. When she smiled, her face expressed great love and tenderness. Her nose was a significant feature of a remarkable face; its nobility signalized a leader and commander. Her bearing was dignified. Her hands, frequently extended in a gesture of giving, were small, slender, delicate. Her eyes, which changed from blue to gray and occasionally to a deep violet as the expression on her face varied, were large and luminous. Her hair, once a dark chestnut hue, had turned to a crown of silvery white.

Of medium height, slender in form, she wore a gown of purple silk covered with black lace. Upon her head was a bonnet in perfect harmony with the dress; upon her breast, a beautiful cross of diamonds, a gift from a student. As a Daughter of the American Revolution, she wore her badge of ruby and diamonds, a gift from another of her many loving students. *The Boston Herald* said of her personal appearance, "She was the picture of health and energy for a lady of her years." At this time Mrs. Eddy was seventy-six years old.

When she concluded her address Mrs. Eddy seated herself on the veranda and listened attentively to the other speakers. Among them, it was my privilege to be requested by Mrs. Eddy to say a few words. Having only recently awakened to the spiritual significance of Christian Science myself, I made no attempt to delve too deeply into the subject and merely offered my concept of the qualities I thought should characterize those coming into Christian Science.

At the conclusion of the exercises, on Mrs. Eddy's invitation, I was accorded my first interview with the Discoverer and Founder of Christian Science. Her manner was spontaneous and cordial, as she grasped my hand. Although she had given a long address, listened to all the speakers, received many of her students, given interviews to others, yet she appeared as fresh and joyous as at the beginning of the day's activities. There was no appearance of age, no indication of weariness. She radiated alertness. Although this interview was a short one, much was said in a few words. She spoke of the great work waiting to be done, and inquired as to the manner of my coming into Christian Science. Although there had been a number of speakers that day and my remarks had been brief, she had heard everything I had said. "You have struck the very fundamentals of our religion," she said. "If you will be true to those sentiments, you will progress in Christian Science."

CHAPTER XII

IT is only natural and logical that one endowed with the spiritual qualities which inspired Mrs. Eddy could not dwell for long in a community without exercising considerable influence for its betterment. During the nine years that I lived in Concord, I witnessed innumerable instances of Mrs. Eddy's interest in the welfare of her home city. And I do not mean merely an aloof sort of interest that contented itself with kindly expressions and an occasional monetary contribution. No, indeed! Preoccupied as Mrs. Eddy was with the Christian Science movement, she might well have been excused from participating in the local affairs of Concord. But she neither claimed nor desired exemption from civic responsibility, although pressure of work compelled her to forego paying much attention to purely social matters.

It would be impossible to give a complete account of the far-reaching effects of Mrs. Eddy's influence in Concord's development, but they were numerous and always of a highly constructive character.

In 1889, when she first moved to Concord, its only transportation facility available was a single horsecar, which ran, or was supposed to run, at intervals of one hour, on Main Street only. The town boasted a few blocks of cobblestone in the business section as its only street paving. There were but few substantial public buildings. But in January, 1908, when Mrs. Eddy left Concord for

Chestnut Hill, the city had a fine electric car service covering nearly the entire city and suburbs. It possessed a new post office, a beautiful State Library building, a City Hall, a public library, a new courthouse, a new high school, and the finest granite church edifice in the State, costing over two hundred thousand dollars, the gift of Mrs. Eddy and her followers. In place of the few blocks of cobblestone, the city paving in 1908 consisted of about fifty blocks of well-constructed tarred macadam and concrete pavements. Mrs. Eddy's residence in Concord directly contributed to these improvements, as well as to increased business in her native State.

At the close of the nineteenth century, although the movement for good roads had not yet reached New Hampshire, Mrs. Eddy saw that the improvement of the roads of Concord was an imperative need. Indeed, the main thoroughfares leading into the city were in such poor condition that in the spring of 1899, a farmer with a light load became stalled in the mire near the entrance to Pleasant View, and at times it was hardly safe for Mrs. Eddy to take her daily drive. She therefore petitioned the Mayor to take action, and a notice to that effect appeared in the *Concord Evening Monitor* of March 15, 1899. But Mrs. Eddy did more than advocate better highways; she started the fund for good roads by offering the Concord city government five thousand dollars, which she later increased to eight thousand, for the macadamizing of Pleasant Street. Her plan, in accord with a survey made by the city engineer, was welcomed by the leading citizens.

Strange as it may seem, an attempt on the part of a few ill-advised individuals was made to defeat her proposed improvement. Mrs. Eddy was surprised, but she was not to be thwarted in her efforts for improved thoroughfares. In spite of threats that a lawsuit would result, she took personal charge of the undertaking, engaged an expert engineer of long experience, and paid his salary and expenses from her own pocket. Her friends at once rallied to her support, and the newspapers published just and fair articles, clearly setting forth the situation.

The opposition soon proved futile and the *Concord Evening Monitor* of September 13, 1899, announced: "The regular monthly meeting of the city government for September was held on Tuesday afternoon. . . .

"The Pleasant Street grade controversy was settled, the board promptly established a grade which . . . had [been] agreed upon." The much-needed improvement was carried forward as Mrs. Eddy had planned.

By the summer of 1906, as a result of Mrs. Eddy's initiative, additional improvements were made in the highways of Concord. But State Street, one of the leading residential streets, on which were located the State Capitol building, the Christian Science church, and many other prominent public buildings, still remained unimproved, and Mrs. Eddy addressed a letter to the citizens of Concord, which was published in the papers of June 21, 1906, and read in part:

Our picturesque city greatly needs improved streets. May I

ask in behalf of the public this favor of our city government, namely:—to macadamize a portion of Warren street and to macadamize State street throughout?

Her appeal to the Concord citizens bore immediate fruit. Upon the publication of this letter, certain of her students, at an expense of three thousand dollars, arranged to have concrete pavement put down upon Warren Street for four blocks. Expressions of interest and co-operation came from other citizens, including Governor Rollins, who wrote to Mrs. Eddy:

Dear Madam: Noticing your very generous offer to the city of Concord, I have written the *Monitor* a letter making some suggestions on the subject which I feel certain will meet your approval. I consider it useless to lay a good pavement on State Street, unless the stone teams can be made to go elsewhere.

Mrs. Eddy agreed with Governor Rollins that the improvements made in Concord highways should be maintained. *The Boston Herald* of August 8, 1906, reported the matter in part as follows:

Through the suggestion of Mrs. Mary Baker Eddy, discoverer and founder of Christian Science, and by vote of the Concord city government tonight, the capital city of the Granite state is to have, in the improvement of State street, one of the finest avenues in New Hampshire. This improvement is the direct result of a request to the city government by Mrs. Eddy, and the generous action of her friends, who have offered to bear half of the expense of concreting one of the city's leading and most beautiful thoroughfares.

Throughout her life Mrs. Eddy was a humanitarian. But her loving activities were not confined to the Cause which she founded, or to her own followers. Her love, like the fragrance of a flower, went forth impartially to the whole world. A few among the many institutions and causes blessed by her benefactions were the following: New Hampshire Historical Society; Young Men's Christian Association; Police Department; Newspaper Writers' Home; San Francisco earthquake sufferers; the New Hampshire State Building at the Jamestown Exposition. The scope of Mrs. Eddy's humanitarian work during a single year may be gathered from figures which she quoted in a letter to me on March 29, 1899: "Recent charities of mine demanded unexpectedly will take my spare change this year. I calculate not less than $15,000 is required to meet them."

Mrs. Eddy's friendly interest was extended not only to Concord; she was glad to lend her practical support to the advancement of her native State of New Hampshire as well. On February 12, 1904, *The Daily Patriot* reported her gift of one thousand dollars to the St. Louis Exposition Fund:

The *Patriot* was very pleased to be able to announce yesterday that the Rev. Mary Baker G. Eddy has offered the sum of $1,000 towards the $15,000 which the commissioners deem sufficient for the creditable representation of New Hampshire at the St. Louis Exposition.

The generous donation speaks volumes for the public-spiritedness of this woman. There are many in New Hampshire just as well able to give, and there are thousands who would be infinitely more justified in giving. The only motive which inspires this act on her part must be her abiding love for the State, and her desire to see New Hampshire in a fitting place among the galaxy of States, as they will appear at the greatest exposition ever held in America.[1]

[1] The plan to have a New Hampshire exhibit was later abandoned.

When "Old Home Week" was first instituted in New Hampshire in 1899, Mrs. Eddy entered heartily into the plans of Governor Rollins for making it a success. She purchased a great many of the "Old Home Week" stamps, appropriately designed for the occasion, and she wrote a personal letter to the Concord papers, cordially endorsing the "Old Home Week" plan. When it was proposed to build a suitable auditorium in Concord to accommodate the throngs which might gather on this and like occasions, she further expressed her interest by a contribution of twelve hundred dollars. Concerning this gift the *Concord Evening Monitor* wrote:

The Rev. Mary Baker Eddy's generous addition of $1,200 to the Auditorium Fund, coming as it does so close upon her gift of $5,000 for the macadamizing of Pleasant street, is a new and signal proof of her genuine public spirit; and it is not amiss for us to advert to a communication which was printed in The Monitor some ten years ago, at the time when Mrs. Eddy first took up her residence in Concord, in which the writer predicted that Mrs. Eddy's residence here would be productive of good to the community. . . .

Christian Science Hall, with Mrs. Eddy's permission, was decorated with flags and bunting. From Boston came a goodly number of Christian Scientists, in response to their Leader's invitation to lend their support to the first "Old Home Week" celebration. The *Boston Traveler,* in its "Old Home Week Supplement," devoted some four pages to a history of the Discoverer and Founder of Christian Science and her Cause, which I had the honor of preparing.

For Dartmouth College, from which her brother Albert

had been graduated, Mrs. Eddy cherished a warm regard, and when the call came for funds to rebuild old Dartmouth Hall, destroyed by fire, she responded with a check for one thousand dollars.

Education and the advancement of learning had always been valued highly by Mrs. Eddy, and her interest took tangible form in her support of the building program of the New Hampton Literary and Biblical Institution, at that time considered one of the finest academies in New Hampshire. When Governor Quinby of New Hampshire sent an appeal for the school, Mrs. Eddy asked many questions about the work of the academy and its building activities, and when she learned of the praiseworthy character of the institution, she asked what she ought to give. I suggested five hundred dollars. She replied, "No, I think I will send a thousand dollars," and she instructed me to give Calvin Frye her message. This gift, made in the spring of 1910, indicated Mrs. Eddy's continuing and sincere interest in her beloved State, even when she was no longer a resident.

Mrs. Eddy's public-spirited interest in her community was clearly illustrated in her attitude toward a proposed Concord State Fair. The Capital of the Granite State had not had a fair for many years, but in 1900, several active businessmen organized a Fair Association and obtained an option on a piece of land which they considered an excellent location. It adjoined the south line of Mrs. Eddy's estate. Under similar circumstances, many would have objected to the proximity, fearing that the crowds might interfere with the privacy of the home, damage property, or create noise and confusion. But Mrs. Eddy put these arguments aside and acted according to her sense of civic service.

Thursday, Governor's Day at the Fair, was largely attended by prominent men, among them the Governor and his staff, United States Senator Henry Blair, and Mrs. Eddy's cousin, the Hon. Henry M. Baker of Bow. On this day, Mrs. Eddy, accompanied by the First Reader of The Mother Church, Judge Septimus J. Hanna, and his wife, was driven to the grounds in her victoria. By special arrangement of the Fair officials, Mrs. Eddy was met at the gate by city and state authorities and escorted around the enclosure by a mounted guard. After acknowledging the applause of the throng as her name was announced over a large megaphone, her carriage was driven to a spot near the center of the grounds from which she could view the proceedings. The trotting horses so delighted her that she stood up in her carriage to clap her hands at the victory of one beautiful trotter. The daring feat of a high diver, who plunged from an elevation of over eighty feet into six feet of water, also specially interested her.

Mrs. Eddy sincerely appreciated the cordial greeting and spontaneous reception accorded her by the people of her home city and native state. Upon receiving a letter expressing the gratification of the management of her appearance on the grounds, and voicing the hope that she might revisit the Fair on future occasions, she wrote to Mr. George H. Moses, late United States Senator, who was then a member of the Fair Association:

I had no intimation and no idea of the kind care and honor that you had in store for me till I met the situation. It was indeed mutually spontaneous, a gentle effusion from the heart of the metropolis of my native state that will never pass from my memory, nor cease to cheer it.

Please find enclosed a check for $1,000, my present gift to the Concord State Fair Association. This small sum is to be applied for aiding the improvement of the exterior of the buildings on the fair grounds—including the cupola on the main building.

By her personal appearance at the Concord Fair, Mrs. Eddy expressed a normal, happy interest in the affairs of her native city. And she refuted the reports of certain out-of-town newspapers that she was incapacitated or even had passed on. The *Concord Evening Monitor* wrote of her visit:

Her presence on the State fair grounds shows the breadth of her interests. "No pent up Utica confines her powers." The demands of her religious duties are exacting but she is concerned with all that makes for the public's highest welfare.

Her cordial patronage of this state enterprise betokens her hearty support of home interests. Though a great religious leader, her religion has not removed her from those concerns which are close at hand. It shows a public spirit, of which the people have many proofs, and is evidence that every worthy public enterprise has her cordial support.

Mrs. Eddy was always alert to discern the human need and prompt in meeting it. In the fall of 1898, when Spanish War soldiers were encamped near Concord, she sent a supply of oranges, grapes, bananas, and peaches to them on one day, and a fish dinner on another day. She contributed one hundred and twenty dollars to the Soldiers' Aid Society, and inquired why suitable tents had not been provided for the troops the night they returned to Concord.

Mrs. Eddy's interest in our fighting forces was nothing new with her. At the opening of the Civil War she made a gift to a soldier that had far-reaching results. Hearing that the son of a poor widow was about to start for the front without a copy of the Bible, she felt a desire to help him. At that time, however, her own income was modest, and her charities to the soldiers and their families had left her on this day with only a dollar in her purse. But the young man's need outweighed her own; one about to risk his life in the service of his country deserved a copy of the Bible, she thought. With her last dollar she bought a copy of the New Testament, gave it to the young man, and thought no more about it. Some time after the close of the war, there came a rap at her door. In the doorway stood a bearded man in a soldier's uniform. "You do not remember me," he said. "I am the soldier to whom you gave a Testament when I left to join my regiment. I have come to thank you for the blessed book, which has always been a help to me, and which saved my life." He then carefully took from his breast pocket a well-worn Testament, which he presented to her. Imbedded between its covers was a leaden bullet.

Christian Science activities in the prisons greatly interested Mrs. Eddy. One of her early talks with me concerned the unfortunates in the county jail and state prison. At her request, I visited the sheriff of the Merrimac County Jail and proposed that Christian Science services be held in the jail on each Sunday afternoon at two o'clock. The sheriff welcomed the plan, remarking that his former efforts in behalf of a service in the jail had met with poor results.[1] When arrangements were completed to hold services, Mrs. Eddy was notified and she replied:

I am glad you have begun the C. S. mission with faith that you can *open* the *prison doors* and set free the captive. God will bless us in this way of His appointing. . . .

Her interest in prison work never flagged. To aid the prisoners in putting off the "old man," she presented the prison with copies of Science and Health, which were immediately put to good use. Frequently Mrs. Eddy received letters from various parts of the Field telling of the good accomplished in the prisons through Christian Science services. So interested was she in having this work made known that she often sent such letters to the Concord church to be read at the Wednesday evening meeting, and then had them forwarded to the Christian Science periodicals for publication. Frequently the expressions of gratitude toward Mrs. Eddy were touching. The prisoners in the New Hampshire State Prison presented her with a wicker chair they had made themselves. In the middle of its back they had woven a cross and crown in color.

Mrs. Eddy held aloft a high ideal for her own sex, in

[1] The sheriff said that one of the good old saints of the city who had undertaken to hold services some time previous had confided in him that for nearly two years he had addressed the prisoners every Sunday upon the parable of the prodigal son. "Isn't it wonderful how long one can talk on the prodigal son?" the church worker had remarked. The following week, the sheriff went on to say, a committee from the prisoners called for him and asked what they had done to deserve such punishment. "Put us all in dark cells, feed us on bread and water," they begged, "but don't torment us any longer with the prodigal son."

religion, in social welfare, and in statesmanship. Even in her girlhood, she had been active in worthy causes, taking a vital interest in the slavery question, and in the movement for temperance. In thanking Clara Louise Burnham for an article written about the Discoverer of Christian Science, Mrs. Eddy wrote: "Our sex seems to be needed at this period to lift the darkness and to cheer the faithful sentinels at their posts of love and duty. God sustains you and will bless you in just this way."

Under her inspired guidance and able direction, the Christian Science movement was rapidly becoming well known outside the borders of the United States, and in 1907 she was officially recognized for her distinguished services as Founder of Christian Science, when the French Government bestowed upon her the decoration of *Officier d'Académie*. The Diploma of Honor was sent by the French Government to Dr. William H. Tolman, Commissioner General of the American section of the Paris International Book and Paper Exposition, and to Pleasant View came Dr. and Mrs. Tolman to make the presentation in person. While waiting to be introduced, Dr. Tolman expressed his appreciation of the privilege accorded him and his gratitude that the French Government had bestowed an honor so worthily.

Her interest in the welfare of the children of Concord endeared her to many parents. Learning of the lack of adequate footwear among the school children of the poor, she arranged for each child, whose parents were unable to supply the need, to be provided with a pair of winter shoes. With her usual clearheaded business methods, she selected as her agent one of the leading shoe merchants of the city, who had the respect and confidence of the community. On the day of the State Fair known as Children's Day, all the children were admitted free of charge and Mrs. Eddy's representative presented coupons, redeemable at the store of the merchant, to those children who, after investigation, had been selected to receive them. Many were the letters of gratitude that came to Mrs. Eddy, and genuine was the appreciation of her thoughtfulness. So successful was the plan of distribution, and so great was the need, that she continued her gifts to the children of Concord for several years. On August 27, 1902, *The Daily Patriot* printed the following account of the distribution:

Children . . . appeared at the store of W. A. Thompson, this morning, to receive the shoes for which they received orders at the Fair Grounds yesterday, and [from] the happiness upon each little face as the owner went forth wearing the shoes, it was very plain that nothing is more profitable than the making of others happy.

The shoes distributed were of a very substantial make and they will give a splendid service, and, beyond a doubt, this is what Mrs. Eddy desired in requesting that the little children of the city be given this substantial evidence of her love and affection for them.

Heretofore the children had the shoes tied up and carried them away, but this year, Mr. Thompson asked that each child have the shoes put on in the store, and . . . go forth wearing them.

The selection was made with great care and thoroughness. One day Mrs. Eddy took satisfaction in showing me the records of the distribution. Every pair of shoes was accounted for, the record showing the kind of shoe presented, the name of the recipient, and his address. Children had been sent by the Salvation Army and by other organizations. Mrs. Eddy's agent wrote: "Every case has been investigated, and you will see by the enclosed report that 205 needy ones have been provided for. In our investigation we found several older persons who were in actual need. These we provided for in your name." Among the children receiving shoes were not only native Americans, but French, Irish, Scandinavians, and other nationalities, without regard to race, color, or religion.

Mrs. Eddy's love included animals and birds as well as human beings. And birds and animals felt the love she radiated and responded to it. Once when riding on a streetcar, a large St. Bernard dog entered, and coming straight to Mrs. Eddy, confidingly placed its head in her lap. On another occasion, one afternoon, she returned home from a walk in Concord with four of these great dogs escorting her, as if to serve as her guard of honor. Horses obeyed her slightest word, and when frightened were quickly calmed by her gentle voice.

A pleasant, friendly relationship existed between Mrs. Eddy and the churches in Concord. Many loving expressions of helpfulness were made on both sides. When one of the buildings of a neighboring community of Shakers was destroyed by fire, Mrs. Eddy was prompt to respond to Governor Rollins' call for donations, with a check for one hundred dollars. Hearing that the Methodist Church in Bow, her birthplace, was in need of a bell, Mrs. Eddy asked her cousin, the Hon. Henry M. Baker, to investigate, and upon his recommendation donated for the church belfry a beautifully toned bell.

The loving friendliness of the Concord churches toward Mrs. Eddy was indicated by the kindly offer which came from two of them at a time when this neighborliness was greatly appreciated. Christian Science Hall had to be torn down, for a new church building was to be erected on the same site. When the Episcopalians heard that the congregation must find a temporary home during this period, they kindly extended the use of their parish house. The Unitarians expressed a like friendliness, and the Christian Scientists were grateful to accept the offer of their church building for Sunday afternoon services. So appreciative was Mrs. Eddy of this kindly courtesy that on Christmas Day, 1903, she sent a letter of Christmas greeting and her check for three hundred dollars to the Unitarian Church.

"Students are advised by the author to be charitable and kind," wrote Mrs. Eddy, "not only towards differing forms of religion and medicine, but to those who hold these differing opinions."[1] This was the rule from which she herself never departed. Both Protestants and Roman Catholics of Concord appreciated her impartial benevolence, and in their love for fair play recognized that she was a public-spirited citizen and a consistent Christian. In her plans for the city's betterment, and in regard to legislation concerning Christian Science which came before municipal or state legislative bodies, she invariably

[1] Science and Health, p. 444.

received kindly consideration from Roman Catholic as well as Protestant citizens, and could count on their just and fair-minded support. Early in January of 1903, a hostile member of the legislature introduced a bill which was intended to outlaw the practice of Christian Science in New Hampshire. But another group, which included some Roman Catholic members of the legislature, immediately arose to defeat such a purpose. The bill was brought before the committee on Monday, and on Tuesday the committee voted it "inexpedient to legislate." On the following day, the author of the bill arose in the legislature and complained that he had not been treated fairly. Although his appeals won the sympathy of some of the legislative members, one of the leading Democrats arose and maintained that the committee had acted wisely in declaring it "inexpedient to legislate," and remarked, "Mrs. Eddy and her followers are among the best citizens of New Hampshire and the bill is an insult to these same citizens." He then moved that the report of the committee be adopted and that the bill be thrown out. The author of this motion was an ardent Roman Catholic, who throughout remained a friend to Mrs. Eddy, and kindly in his attitude toward Christian Science.

Knowing her sympathy for all religions, the editor of the *Concord Evening Monitor*, at the death of Pope Leo XIII on July 20, 1903, requested that Mrs. Eddy write a tribute to his memory. The tribute, reprinted on page 294 of "The First Church of Christ, Scientist, and

Miscellany," demonstrated that however much Mrs. Eddy's views may have differed from the creeds and doctrines of other churches, for the individual members of all denominations she had only love and good will.

Mrs. Eddy was essentially a citizen of the world. The truth she voiced was for all mankind; the hosts who followed her include men and women of every nation. Those of us closely associated with her were impressed with the universality of her work. There was nothing narrow or insular about the Founder of the Christian Science movement. She had a breadth of vision that was world-wide. Her love was broad and expanding, encircling all mankind. She made it clear to us that in this world "no man liveth to himself," and that the affairs of each individual are so intertwined with the affairs of his brother that isolation is an impossibility.

On the question of peace and war she had much to say. When Portsmouth, a leading city in her native State of New Hampshire, was chosen for the peace conference for the settlement of the Japanese-Russian War, I remember how pleased she was, and at its final adjudication she requested the chimes in her Concord church to ring out the glad news.

But Mrs. Eddy was in no sense a pacifist. I never heard her voice a word in behalf of pacifism, but she did often quote the apostle's words: "Fight the good fight of faith, lay hold on eternal life." And although she was strongly in favor of conciliation and arbitration, she did not counsel neutrality or pacifism when the safety and honor of her country demanded strength and firmness. In *The Boston*

Herald of March, 1898, she clearly set forth her views when she wrote:

I will say I can see no other way of settling difficulties between individuals and nations than by means of their wholesome tribunals, equitable laws, and sound, well-kept treaties. . . . But if our nation's rights or honor were seized, every citizen would be a soldier and woman would be armed with power girt for the hour.[1]

In my twelve years' experience, I do not recall a single instance in which I found Mrs. Eddy to be neutral. On questions of public policy, she beheld the moral issue as paramount, the welfare of all mankind as the primary issue, and on such matters she was never neutral. Through communion with the one Mind, she sought a clear concept of the right and the wrong of each vital question. Then she took her stand definitely for what she believed to be right. From her girlhood, she had never been afraid to declare her views and to adhere firmly to the stand she had prayerfully taken. Arguments of expediency or popularity failed to intimidate her. She recognized her duty "to help support a righteous government,"[2] and by her action she demonstrated the support of righteousness and justice in government wherever found.

Mrs. Eddy's love for the nations of the world did not lessen her love for her native land. Every word she spoke along these lines to her household, every message she gave to the world, was on fire with loyalty and love for her own country. Her counsel and admonition made of her students better citizens and patriots as well as better men and women. In messages to her church, in contributions

[1] Miscellany, p. 277.   [2] Miscellany, p. 276.

to the newspapers, she admonished her followers to pray for the welfare and prosperity of the nation and for guidance and protection of the officials connected with the administration of her government.

In 1898, when the United States was at war with Spain, she wrote, in her annual message to The Mother Church:

> In your peaceful homes remember our brave soldiers, whether in camp or in battle. Oh, may their love of country, and their faithful service thereof, be unto them life-preservers! May the divine Love succor and protect them, as at Manila, where brave men, led by the dauntless Dewey, and shielded by the power that saved them, sailed victoriously through the jaws of death and blotted out the Spanish squadron.
>
> Great occasion have we to rejoice that our nation, which fed her starving foe,—already murdering her peaceful seamen and destroying millions of her money,—will be as formidable in war as she has been compassionate in peace.[1]

There was no weak pacifism in her position, but a love of country and a support of those policies which she believed to be the nearest right under the circumstances.

When a crisis arose in the world's affairs, Mrs. Eddy did not hesitate to speak and to act. She never failed to add the weight of her influence and power to the side of human welfare, to the side of right and justice. In 1908, when the controversy between Great Britain and Germany with regard to the sea power was becoming acute, reverberations were heard on both sides of the Atlantic. Germany set out to build a big navy, England counterbuilt to increase her sea forces. Under the circumstances, President Theodore Roosevelt, who earnestly

[1] "Christian Science *versus* Pantheism," p. 14.

advocated an increase in our country's armament, declared in his Message of April 14, 1908, to Congress:

There is a rank due to the United States among nations which will be withheld, if not absolutely lost, by the reputation of weakness. If we desire to avoid insult, we must be able to repel it; if we desire to secure peace, one of the most powerful instruments of our rising prosperity, it must be known that we are at all times ready for war.

There was much controversy and opposition on the part of pacifists and isolationists. During the course of the controversy, Mary Baker Eddy issued a statement clearly setting forth her views as to what she believed the proper position for her country to take. She wrote in the *Christian Science Sentinel* of April 11, 1908:

For many years I have prayed daily that there be no more war, no more barbarous slaughtering of our fellow-beings; prayed that all the peoples on earth and the islands of the sea have one God, one Mind; love God supremely, and love their neighbor as themselves.

National disagreements can be, and should be, arbitrated wisely, fairly; and fully settled.

It is unquestionable, however, that at this hour the armament of navies is necessary, for the purpose of preventing war and preserving peace among nations.[1]

In this international crisis, Mrs. Eddy was neither apathetic nor neutral. She took a definite stand. Nor was this all. Not content to leave the matter there, she took steps to see that her words were read where they would do the most good. She instructed her Publication Committee to make a wide distribution of the *Sentinel* containing her statement on armaments throughout the

[1] Miscellany, p. 286.

United States and Great Britain, among members of the legislative bodies, and other prominent men.

Mrs. Eddy was always alert to world problems. She saw clearly that the difficulties and troubles of international disputes can never be healed by ignoring their seeming existence. Mrs. Eddy knew and taught her followers that an erroneous situation must be faced and positive steps taken to correct it. Apropos of this, on September 15, 1909, she called the members of her household into her study and asked us to read Luke 22, for therein was portrayed the events of the hour. She said we were to see in the words, not desolation, but consolation. The task before us was to put aside the claims of the flesh and to put on the spiritual. This would give us plenty of employment.

The author of Science and Health knew that the way to universal peace must begin in the consciousness of the individual.

An important step toward universal peace foreseen by Mrs. Eddy was the establishment of cordial relations between Great Britain and the United States expressed in Mrs. Eddy's own words, "Unite your battle-plan." These historic words were written in the year 1898, following the formal declaration of war between the United States and Spain, when there appeared in *The London Chronicle* a poem entitled "Greeting from England." When this poem was brought to Mrs. Eddy's attention, she was inspired to write her prophetic utterance, "The United States to Great Britain." Not only does this poem disclose her as a loyal citizen of her native land, but the metaphysical significance of her words reveals her as a friend of all nations.

Recent events taking place in world affairs appear to fulfill the prophetic words contained in the first and last verses of her poem[1]:

> Hail, brother! fling thy banner
>   To the billows and the breeze;
> We proffer thee warm welcome
>   With our hand, though not our knees.
>
> . . . .
>
> Brave Britain, blest America!
>   Unite your battle-plan;
> Victorious, all who live it,—
>   The love for God and man.

[1] Poems, p. 10.

CHAPTER XIII

O N the Sunday afternoon of January 26, 1908, Mrs. Eddy and the members of her household drove to the railway station at Concord and boarded the special train waiting to carry them to Boston. A Pullman car had been provided for Mrs. Eddy, another coach for the members of her household, and in addition a baggage car and engine.

Wearing a gray suit, sable cape, small gray toque trimmed with purple and white ostrich plumes, and the customary white kid gloves, Mrs. Eddy entered the drawing room in the Pullman car, accompanied by Mrs. Laura E. Sargent and Calvin Frye. Her cheerfulness impressed us all, although doubtless it was not an easy experience for her to leave the dear home at Pleasant View.

Not a single word had appeared in the Boston or the New York press relative to Mrs. Eddy's change of residence, although any newspaper fortunate enough to print the news would have considered it a great "scoop." As a matter of fact, a keen reporter of *The Boston Globe* surmised that something was in the wind and carefully watched all freight coming from Concord to Boston. Discovering that trunks, furniture, and boxes were being sent from Pleasant View to Chestnut Hill, he called upon the editor-in-chief of the Christian Science periodicals, and, informing him that his newspaper had absolute proof that Mrs. Eddy was moving to Greater Boston, asked for an official confirmation of the news, and for additional data for publication. Surprised at this announcement, the editor-in-chief presented Mrs. Eddy's side of the situation to the reporter, and so sincere was this appeal that he was persuaded to withhold the information until after Mrs. Eddy arrived at Chestnut Hill. This act of kindness was greatly appreciated by Mrs. Eddy.

Although there was no direct railway connection between Concord, New Hampshire, and Chestnut Hill, Massachusetts, through the courtesy of the railroad officials special arrangements conveyed Mrs. Eddy, without change of cars, directly to the Chestnut Hill station, where her carriage and coachman, sent on ahead, were awaiting her.

The news of Mrs. Eddy's departure from Concord traveled faster than her train; consequently when she arrived at her new home, about five in the afternoon, she found awaiting her a large delegation of newspaper men and photographers. John Salchow, her faithful helper, saw the crowd of curious onlookers, and before anyone could make a move he had gathered Mrs. Eddy up in his arms and carried her out of the newspaper men's reach to the second floor of the house.

In the details of her new home and its furnishings, Mrs. Eddy took special interest. She was very fond of an old-fashioned whatnot, now in the pink room at Chestnut Hill, upon which were placed photographs, gifts, and mementos from students and others, among them a miniature gold pick and shovel which Mrs. Eddy's grandsons had presented to her. Among the few ornaments which were chosen by Mrs. Eddy herself were two statuettes, one representing George and the dragon, and the other David, and these were given prominent places.

At Chestnut Hill, the members of Mrs. Eddy's household lived a normal and happy life. A few of them took an interest in the wild flowers and animals on the estate and in the neighboring country. Within ten minutes' walk of the Chestnut Hill residence, one worker identified one hundred and forty varieties of wild flowers; his vest pocket diary for 1910 also listed ninety different species of birds seen during that year. Every one of the secretaries owned a bicycle, and during the very early morning one or more of us would take a short ride through the byways of the neighborhood.

Although each of us had his special hours of work, yet never was there a moment when we did not hold ourselves in readiness to assume any additional duties that might arise. Our recreational periods, therefore, were usually before 8.30 in the morning, the hour of Mrs. Eddy's arrival at her study, and between one and two in the afternoon, the hour when she took her daily drive.

Some of the workers were interested in astronomy and occasionally spent a pleasant evening on the roof of the Chestnut Hill residence, easily reached by a flight of stairs from the upper story. It was not long before a telescope was placed on the upper story, so arranged that it could easily be transported to the roof on clear, starry evenings. One member of the family procured some works on astronomy, and before the summer was over many of the

Chestnut Hill

"she arrived at her new home about five in the afternoon"

little group could readily point out the chief constellations and the stars of greater magnitude in the heavens. Only occasionally did the secretaries have time to devote an evening to this recreation, for they were usually too much occupied.

After Mrs. Eddy's arrival at Chestnut Hill, she carried through the tremendous undertaking of launching the daily newspaper, *The Christian Science Monitor,* itself a major achievement for the Cause and for the world, yet for the most part her work during those last three years did not consist of such acts of outward organization as had occupied her continuously for nearly half a century. The great work of founding her church, establishing the denominational literature, writing the By-Laws of her church, forming and overseeing the various institutional activities of the Christian Science movement, was for the most part accomplished. Now her work lay along a different line. It was more unseen by the world, and scarcely understood by the most advanced student of Christian Science. She once remarked that she led such a lonely life. That remark was not understood by her hearers at the time, but more than one of them has since understood it. She was spiritually far in advance of any human being on this earth. She had the leadership of a great Cause in her charge, and there was no one to whom she could turn for counsel, comfort, or encouragement. But her students and workers turned to her for guidance in the sober business of conducting the movement, and although she continued, during those years, to grant interviews to the various officials of the church, yet she endeavored to turn them away from her human personality, and gently to lead them to God, who would guide, care for, and lead both their individual lives and the Cause for which they labored.

The members of her household she constantly sought to instruct in the way of spiritual progress. Often, to aid us in performing our duties, she would dispel the spiritual dullness with illuminating statements of truth. She taught us that we should know and realize that one does not grow weary in doing good, when one truly knows what good is; then will the claims of material sense fall away. "In my childhood," she said, "I was taught that religion was a solemn, altogether dolorous affair. Now I know that it should be just the opposite—religion should beget joy and good cheer." One day a member of the household received this note from Mrs. Eddy: "Choose ye this day whom ye will serve if it be God, let it be God that is if it be Spirit let it be Spirit and *not matter*. Read . . . at the table to-day."

The note was read, at her direction, and it served its purpose, awakening the members of the household to the need of more spiritual alertness. At another time, she lifted our thought by telling us that the best way to meet evil arguments is to realize the holy sense of God as All, and know there is no other mind. Nobody can suffer or cause suffering for speaking the truth; nobody can affect others through a lie. Again, she counseled us to take the ground that disease cannot be formed in our unconscious or conscious thought. God, divine Love, gives us all our thoughts. There is but one Mind and all thought comes to us from that Mind, and goes forth from us from that Mind.

Mrs. Eddy taught us that weather conditions are not beyond God's control, and that they can be corrected through right prayer. She made it clear that Christian Scientists are not to attempt to control or govern the weather. We should know that God governs the weather and no other influence can be brought to bear on it. She said we are to be particularly watchful to guard against any disastrous effects of storms.

Other Christian churches also offer prayer when adverse weather conditions prevail. In 1930, during a severe summer drought, one State which was suffering great damage called all Christians to pray for rain. Notice to this effect was sent to all daily papers in that State.

While on duty at Chestnut Hill one evening, a member of the household unwittingly overheard Mrs. Eddy pray aloud. Her petition was scientific, orderly in procedure, and precise in choice of language. It contained no request for a special blessing for health, comfort, or prosperity for herself or her Cause, but was a beautiful declaration of the power of Spirit to bless all mankind. She affirmed that there was no lack of God's promises for His offspring, and declared God's presence, hourly and momentarily. Her audible declaration of the power of good recalled the truth that real prayer is at the very heart of Christian Science.

Not only was Mrs. Eddy called upon throughout the years to bear the burden and tremendous responsibility of leading the Christian Science Cause, but in addition she had to work out her own salvation, and to contend with personal problems in her experience. To the very last she was as mentally alert, as keenly intelligent, and as vigorous in mental power as she was throughout her long career. During those last years, the quality of her writing, the spiritual power of her thinking, and the keenness of her grasp on the problems of the Cause were unsurpassed by her former achievements. Never did she relinquish, either tacitly or outwardly, the watchful interest in her own personal affairs, or her leadership of the world-wide Cause which she founded.

As the years advanced, Mrs. Eddy was vigilant in working for herself, turning the truth upon whatever suggestion presented itself. One morning as we gathered in the study at her call, she said that recently in working on the question of sight she had opened the Bible to Luke 18, verse 42, and had realized the true significance of Jesus' words, "Receive thy sight." Then, turning to me, she said, "Hand me the newspaper." I complied with her request. Without glasses, and holding the newspaper at a normal distance, she then read without hesitation an editorial on "Progress in the Philippines."

It was during those last years at Chestnut Hill that a sore trial arose in the schism which threatened to split a large metropolitan church, as the result of the disloyalty of one of Mrs. Eddy's early students. This student, who had been very dear to her, now arrogantly set herself up in subtle opposition to the teacher who had endeavored to guide and guard her footsteps throughout the years.

Mrs. Eddy struggled for a long time to rescue this misguided student from the brink of the precipice, but in vain. After a painful period of disruption in this branch church, the schism was at length healed, the members declared their love for Mrs. Eddy, their loyalty to The Christian Science Board of Directors and to the Manual of The Mother Church, and the disloyal member was excommunicated from The Mother Church.

Mrs. Eddy's sure and effective handling of the mental malpractice which threatened this branch church testified to the virility of her thought and to her capacity for expediting the affairs of the movement at this period. At times she had mighty wrestlings with error. But she was faithful in applying the truth to whatever argument assailed her, and she never swerved from the path in which her feet had been set. One morning she quoted the seventeenth verse of the eleventh chapter of I Corinthians, and then, revealing a bit of her struggle, she added, as I afterward wrote down:

I had a hard time last night, but I am only the better for it. Why? Because every trial of our faith lifts us higher. We rise by what we demonstrate.

I want you all to talk less and realize more. The devil gets after us when we talk, but he is foiled when we demonstrate the truth. A musician might talk harmony tones and semi-tones, but when I asked him to play, suppose he failed? His words would only emphasize his failure. Don't discourage me by talking so much.

One day, in speaking of the general belief in the power of age and death, Mrs. Eddy said that since all is Life, God, there is no old age and death. Death is an enemy which is to be overcome, not submitted to. We have no authority for believing that death is a friend, or a steppingstone to immortality, but we do have Biblical authority for overcoming it. Paul said, "The last enemy that shall be destroyed is death." The way to destroy a lie is to tell the truth about it. The way to destroy the enemy death is to realize its powerlessness in the face of the ever-presence of Life, Truth, and Love.

One evening, in January, 1910, she said, "I love to think that my life is hid with Christ in God—with Truth in divine Love. Every night I say over to myself this little verse of the hymn:

> "The Spirit's sweet control
> Freely we will confess,—
> Fly to Thine out-stretched arms of love,
> And there find health and rest."
>
> M. J. H. Zink

Mrs. Eddy habitually relied upon the power of God to meet her every need. He was her one and only and her great Physician. I am in a position to state that Mary Baker Eddy never relied on the use of narcotics or drugs. For nearly three years, as a member of her household at Chestnut Hill, I saw her not only daily, but often several times during the day. My service was of a varied nature and brought me in close contact with her. Never did I see her indulge in drugs of any kind. Neither did she nor any member of her household use tea, coffee, or tobacco. All, in every time of need, faithfully utilized the power of God, through prayer, for healing. With other members of her household, I was with Mrs. Eddy at the end, and

"Mary Baker Eddy's true memorial"

her passing away was peaceful and serene. Her last written words, "God is my life," were in full harmony with the life and deeds of this inspired woman to whom Spirit was ever supreme.

In June, 1891, nineteen years before she left us, our Leader sent to the Massachusetts Metaphysical College Association this message, which reads in part:

My Beloved Students:—You may be looking to see me in my accustomed place with you, but this you must no longer expect. When I retired from the field of labor, it was a departure, socially, publicly, and finally, from the routine of such material modes as society and our societies demand. Rumors are rumors,—nothing more. I am still with you on the field of battle, taking forward marches, broader and higher views, and with the hope that you will follow. . . .

All our thoughts should be given to the absolute demonstration of Christian Science. You can well afford to give me up, since you have in my last revised edition of Science and Health your teacher and guide.[1]

This is the message which was read at the close of the morning service in The Mother Church on the Sunday following Mrs. Eddy's passing. "Although these lines were written years ago," the First Reader continued, "they are true today and will continue to be true."

Truly may it be said of Mary Baker Eddy that her works do follow her. Although a memorial in her honor was erected in Mt. Auburn Cemetery, Cambridge, Massachusetts, a memorial which in its form and beauty points to immortality and the uninterrupted continuity of life, yet Mary Baker Eddy's true memorial is the church which she founded to perpetuate the healing works of Jesus. "By

[1] "Miscellaneous Writings," pp. 135, 136.

their fruits ye shall know them."[1] The fruits of her life are seen in regenerated lives; in lives brought back from the brink of the grave, saved from the ravages of consuming fears, redeemed from degrading sin and want and misery; in hearts comforted and healed of consuming grief; in lives raised from deepest darkness to the light of renewed hope and joy and courage.

[1] Matthew 7:20.

CHAPTER XIV

A TRUE appraisal of a great character in history is not always gained at once. It often happens that considerable time must elapse for the world to reach a state of understanding sufficient to perceive true greatness. But if the world is to receive the message of Christian Science which Mrs. Eddy brought, then it must obtain a true estimate of the messenger. Christian Scientists are convinced that just as the advent of Jesus proved the "first coming" of the Christ, so are they certain that Mary Baker Eddy's discovery of Christian Science fulfilled the prophecy of the "second coming." And there is ample Biblical authority to substantiate the conviction that Mrs. Eddy was God's messenger to this age through whom the message of the "second coming" was revealed to the world.

It is significant that Jesus considered it of the utmost importance that his disciples should perceive his direct relationship with the Father. In the fourteenth chapter of John occur these words of the Master: "Believest thou not that I am in the Father, and the Father in me? the words that I speak unto you I speak not of myself: but the Father that dwelleth in me, he doeth the works. Believe me that I am in the Father, and the Father in me: or else believe me for the very works' sake."

He knew that this correct perception was necessarily spiritual, and that without it, the works his disciples might perform would be limited. He also knew how impossible it was for those unenlightened spiritually to see him as other than the son of Joseph the carpenter. Jesus was well aware how difficult it was for his contemporaries to see an inspired prophet in a familiar figure, but he also knew that his disciples must see him aright for their own spiritual growth. Hence his insistence on this point of recognition, as revealed in the sixteenth chapter of Matthew: "Whom do men say that I the Son of man am? And they said, Some say that thou art John the Baptist: some, Elias; and others, Jeremias, or one of the prophets. He saith unto them, But whom say ye that I am? And Simon Peter answered and said, Thou art the Christ, the Son of the living God. And Jesus answered and said unto him, Blessed art thou, Simon Bar-jona: for flesh and blood hath not revealed it unto thee, but my Father which is in heaven."

Jesus did not long for his disciples' recognition of him as the Son of God for any personal reason. Far from it. No man ever lived who sought personal homage less. No man on earth was ever freer than Jesus from any thought of self-aggrandizement, yearning for fame, position, or possessions. His great yearning for recognition of his sonship was born of his desire that mankind should see God's love reflected through him. For Jesus knew that if men could not behold him as the Son of God, demonstrating the Christ, they could not possibly perceive the Father. This is one reason why he pleaded with his disciples to believe that the Father was in him "for the very works' sake."

He discerned that those who lacked spiritual vision might have difficulty in recognizing him as representing the Christ; but even the dullest among them could not fail to acknowledge the healings he had performed. And how else could those works be explained but as the demonstrations of the allness of God, thus proving Jesus' sonship with the Father?

In the fourth chapter of Luke we read: "Verily I say unto you, No prophet is accepted in his own country." This was the state of thought which confronted Jesus; this, too, in certain instances, was the problem which Mary Baker Eddy had to face. To those who had known Mary Baker on her father's farm at Bow and watched her grow from childhood to maturity, it was difficult for them to acknowledge her as the Discoverer, Founder, and Leader of a great religious movement. And even though her daily life and conduct compelled them to acknowledge her goodness, patience, and love, many of her closest acquaintances and relatives failed to understand her God-ordained mission. Although there is Biblical precedent for this state of human consciousness, the fact remains, however, that it is absolutely essential to the understanding and demonstration of Christian Science to see its Discoverer aright, to recognize her unique position as the revelator of Truth to this age. For it is beyond doubt true that if we do not understand the revelator we cannot correctly understand the revelation.

How necessary it is for Mrs. Eddy's followers to understand her divine office! Not for her glorification or distinction, but solely because seeing her correctly is a necessary step to seeing Truth correctly.

The fact that Mrs. Eddy did not wish her followers to

see God's messenger as a corporeal being, did not mean that she refused to be seen as a distinct individuality, or a defined status, as witness her emphasis on her place as Discoverer, Founder, and Leader of Christian Science.

Christian Science could not be a human invention. It must have originated with God. And the works resulting from Mrs. Eddy's discovery prove its divine origin. Only by divine inspiration could the healings wrought in Christian Science ever have taken place. Only by divine revelation could Mrs. Eddy have brought about her own healing, achieved her epoch-making discovery, written Science and Health, established her church, and revolutionized the thinking of the world.

The healing work established by Mary Baker Eddy not only proves the existence of God, but also the truth contained in the Bible. And to those with eyes to see, there is abundant Scriptural testimony clearly showing Mrs. Eddy's place in Bible prophecy. She made it plain to the members of her household and to all Christian Scientists that it was the truth revealed to her by divine Mind and which found expression through her, that was the Leader of the Christian Science movement, and not a corporeal personality. At her home in Chestnut Hill, Mrs. Eddy was most careful to make this point clear to any new member of the household. She would gather us all together and ask the question, "Do you see me?" The newcomer would reply, "Why, yes, Mrs. Eddy, I see you." Then, ever desirous of diverting attention from her human personality, Mrs. Eddy would gently say, "You see me only in my writings."

This right concept of the Discoverer and Founder of Christian Science was so important to Mrs. Eddy that she frequently repeated it. On one occasion when the Christian Science Publication Committees visited her, at her request I showed some of the members through the house. Later they had a brief audience with Mrs. Eddy, and afterward she gave me this message for them: "You do not see me in person, but you find me in my writings." Again she referred to this important point in her "Letter to a Clergyman"[1]: "We look for the sainted Revelator in his writings, and there we find him. Those who look for me in person, or elsewhere than in my writings, lose me instead of find me."

It was Mrs. Eddy's constant endeavor to turn the thoughts of her followers away from herself as a human personality to the contemplation of the divine revelation that had come to the world from God through her. The discovery of Christian Science signalized the arrival of the Comforter as promised by Jesus, according to John, chapter fourteen: "But the Comforter, which is the Holy Ghost, whom the Father will send in my name, he shall teach you all things. . . ."

For centuries, theologians, Bible students, and Christians of all denominations have been in a state of eager expectancy regarding what is usually referred to as the "second coming." According to popular belief, the "second coming" is generally interpreted as the reappearance of Jesus on earth, and Mrs. Eddy is the first person in history to controvert this theory. She has shown con-

[1] Miscellany, p. 120.

clusively that the "second coming" refers not to the reappearance of the human Jesus, but to the discovery of the Christ, "The divine manifestation of God, which comes to the flesh to destroy incarnate error."[1] Christ, Truth, is the Holy Ghost or divine Comforter which Jesus said would come.

Jesus manifested the "first coming" of the Christ to mankind, and Mary Baker Eddy's discovery of Christian Science (the Comforter) has completely fulfilled the Biblical prophecy of the "second coming." In the first chapter of Genesis we read: "So God created man in his own image, in the image of God created he him; male and female created he them." Here is the implied but unequivocal statement of the fatherhood and motherhood of God. In her spiritual interpretation of the Lord's Prayer on page 16 of Science and Health, Mrs. Eddy refers to "Our Father-Mother God," thus illuminating our understanding by revealing God as Father and Mother, representing the fullness and completeness of His nature. Just as Jesus in the "first coming" revealed the fatherhood of God, so Mrs. Eddy in the "second coming" of the Christ revealed the motherhood of God.

Further proof of the fact that Mary Baker Eddy is God's messenger to this age is fully substantiated by the works resulting from the practice of Christian Science. Jesus said, "By their fruits ye shall know them," and on this basis alone can Christian Science be adequately judged. Since the advent of Jesus no one has ever arisen to interpret his teachings in a manner comparable to

[1] Science and Health, p. 583.

Mrs. Eddy. The healing work of Christian Science which she has given the world provides unassailable evidence of her position as the revelator of the Christ, Truth, to our age. By her works Mary Baker Eddy stands before the world as the one through whom the prophecy of the "second coming" is fulfilled. This "final revelation,"[1] coming through Mrs. Eddy, is "without father, without mother, without descent, having neither beginning of days, nor end of life; but made like unto the Son of God."[2]

Just as Jesus was well aware of his divine mission and supremely confident that his words would endure throughout time, so is there abundant proof that Mary Baker Eddy was thoroughly cognizant of her God-ordained appointment. Otherwise, without the sublime conviction of her Father-Mother's support and ever-presence, she could not have carried out her lifework and conquered the mountainous opposition that attempted to frustrate every step of her progress Spiritward.

As a further illustration of her recognition of her own spiritual status as the inspired Discoverer of Christian Science, we read her words on page 70 of "Retrospection and Introspection." After stating that no one can ever take the place of Jesus, Mrs. Eddy writes: "No person can take the place of the author of Science and Health, the Discoverer and Founder of Christian Science. Each individual must fill his own niche in time and eternity. The second appearing of Jesus is, unquestionably, the spiritual advent of the advancing idea of God, as in Christian Science."

[1] Science and Health, p. 107.   [2] Hebrews 7:3.

The primal cause of all that is, we know, is God, divine Mind, eternal Truth. This primal cause, as clearly indicated, includes fatherhood and motherhood, the masculine and feminine states of consciousness which are typified by the two witnesses, Christ and Christian Science, Christ being made manifest through the manhood of Jesus and Christian Science through the womanhood of Mary Baker Eddy. It is significant that according to Hebrew law at least two witnesses were required to establish a fact. In Deuteronomy we read: "at the mouth of two witnesses, or at the mouth of three witnesses, shall the matter be established." On this point Mrs. Eddy makes this comment on page 346 of "The First Church of Christ, Scientist, and Miscellany": "Science and Health makes it plain to all Christian Scientists that the manhood and womanhood of God have already been revealed in a degree through Christ Jesus and Christian Science, His two witnesses."

Students of the Bible know that in the fifty-third chapter of Isaiah, Christ Jesus is characterized and his works set forth. Of him the prophet writes: "He is despised and rejected of men; a man of sorrows, and acquainted with grief: and we hid as it were our faces from him."

In the fifty-fourth chapter we have the prophecy of the second witness. The sixth verse reads: "For the Lord hath called thee as a woman forsaken and grieved in spirit, . . . saith thy God." Then in the eleventh verse a glowing future is set before this second witness: "O thou afflicted, tossed with tempest, and not comforted, behold, I will lay thy stones with fair colours, and lay thy foundations with sapphires;" and in the thirteenth verse it continues, "all thy children shall be taught of the Lord; and great shall be the peace of thy children." The conclusion in the seventeenth verse is a glorious prophecy: "No weapon that is formed against thee shall prosper; and every tongue that shall rise against thee in judgment thou shalt condemn." How perfectly has this prophecy been fulfilled in Mrs. Eddy's life.

It is in Revelation, the concluding book of the Bible, that the prophecy concerning the fatherhood and motherhood of God, the manhood and womanhood of God's messengers, is completely unveiled. In verse one of the twelfth chapter we read: "And there appeared a great wonder in heaven; a woman clothed with the sun, and the moon under her feet, and upon her head a crown of twelve stars." And in verse five of the same chapter it says: "And she brought forth a man child, who was to rule all nations with a rod of iron: and her child was caught up unto God, and to his throne." The child, of course, is Christian Science.

Chapter ten reads in part: "And I saw another mighty angel come down from heaven, clothed with a cloud: and a rainbow was upon his head, and his face was as it were the sun, and his feet as pillars of fire: and he had in his hand a little book open: and he set his right foot upon the sea, and his left foot on the earth." Apropos of this passage, I remember how pleased Mrs. Eddy was to have a painting of the angel with the little book placed at the head of the stairs on the second floor at Chestnut Hill.

In the tenth chapter of Revelation, verse eight, the prophetic writing continues: "And the voice which I heard from heaven spake unto me again, and said, Go and take the little book which is open in the hand of the angel which standeth upon the sea and upon the earth."

Mrs. Eddy, on pages 558 and 559 of Science and Health, has given us the full meaning of these prophetic words. Of the new evangel she writes, on page 558: "This angel or message which comes from God, clothed with a cloud, prefigures divine Science."

Writing further of this second witness, Mrs. Eddy tells us on page 559 of Science and Health: "This angel had in his hand 'a little book,' open for all to read and understand." And on page 560 of the textbook we are given the true estimate of God's messenger, where Mrs. Eddy writes: " . . . the grand necessity of existence is to gain the true idea of what constitutes the kingdom of heaven in man," and then she adds this important admonition: "This goal is never reached while we hate our neighbor or entertain a false estimate of anyone whom God has appointed to voice His Word." And on the same page: " . . . without a correct sense of its highest visible idea, we can never understand the divine Principle."

No one could serve twelve years under Mrs. Eddy's counsel and instruction without realizing how clearly she recognized her position as prophesied by St. John the Revelator. With superb courage, she braved the severe encounters which the resistance and hatred of the carnal mind persistently enlisted against the spiritual idea presented in Christian Science, for she perceived the fulfillment of the Revelator's prophecy in her own life, and in Christian Science. This is evidenced by her own words: "The twelfth chapter of the Apocalypse, or Revelation of St. John, has a special suggestiveness in connection with the nineteenth century."[1]

Through her fidelity to divine Principle, Mary Baker Eddy was enabled to open the seven-sealed book mentioned in Revelation by means of the spiritual idea revealed in Christian Science. The Apocalyptic vision she elucidated not only in written words, but also in living letters of fire in her own life experience.

As the years pass, Mary Baker Eddy's true position will be more fully recognized and appreciated. As Jesus strove to turn the attention of his disciples away from his corporeality and to open their eyes to his real identity, so did Mrs. Eddy endeavor to turn the thought of her followers away from her personality and to reveal through her writings her true place in spiritual history.

The real identity of God's messenger to this age will be unfolded as mankind seeks to understand it through a study of the Bible and her writings.

[1] Science and Health, p. 559.

INDEX

Farlow, Alfred, 152
Fellowship Committee, 6
Female Bravery, 31
Fields, James T., 93
First Church of Christ, Scientist, Concord, N. H., 96, 110, 115, 119, 120, 121, 122, 148, 166, 177, 178, 186, 192
First Church of Christ, Scientist, and Miscellany, The, 96, 97, 140, 191, 192
  quoted, 8, 9, 47, 94, 102, 117, 118, 123–125, 128, 132, 140, 151, 171, 173, 193, 195, 213, 216
First Members of The Mother Church, 70, 136
Fort Sumter, 30
France, 122
Franconia Notch, N. H., 93
Freemasons' Monthly Magazine, The, 26
French Government, 187
Frye, Calvin A., 58, 59, 107, 121, 166, 169, 170, 182, 198

G

Garfield, President, 70
Gems for You, 92, 93
Georgia, 86
Germany, 164, 194
Gilman, James F., 97, 98
Glover, Major George W., 21–26
Glover, Mary B. (See Eddy, Mary Baker)
Good Templars, 35
Great Britain, 194, 196
Greeley, Horace, 93
Greeting from England (poem), 196

H

Hale, Sarah J., 93
Hanna, Judge Septimus J., 139, 183
Hannover, Germany, 164
Harper's Weekly, 94
Hay, Ella H., 2
Herald of Christian Science, The (Dutch Edition), 101

Herald of Christian Science, The (French Edition), 101
Herald of Christian Science, The (Scandinavian Edition), 101
Herold der Christian Science, Der, 100, 101
Hill, Hon. Isaac, 92
Historical Sketches by Clifford P. Smith, 2
Holmes Academy, 20
Home Forum Page, 106

I

Independence Day, 60, 173
Independent Statesman, 92
"International Series," 144

J

Jackson, Andrew, 18
Jamestown Exposition, 180
Japanese-Russian War, 192
Jesus, 4, 34, 35, 49, 51, 72, 73, 75, 77, 84, 89, 91, 113, 149, 207, 209–211, 213, 216, 219
Jordan Marsh Company, 107

K

Keeley Cure, 4
Kimball, Edward A., 87
Kimball, W. G. C., 160
King, William Rufus, 92
Knapp, Mrs. Flavia S., 5, 6
Knapp, Mr. Ira O., 5

L

Lane, Mr., 92
Lesson-Sermons (See Christian Science Bible Lessons)
Libby prison, 31
Life of Mary Baker Eddy, The, by Sibyl Wilbur, 2
London Chronicle, The, 196
London, England, 56, 57
Lynn, Mass., 6, 33, 35, 37, 38, 42, 44, 47, 54, 68, 135
Lynn Reporter, The, 35

M

Main Street, Concord, N. H., 176
Manchester, N. H., 92
Mary Baker Eddy: A Life Size Portrait by Dr. Lyman P. Powell, 2
Mary B. Glover's Christian Scientists' Home, 68
Masons, 26
Massachusetts, 115
Massachusetts Metaphysical College, 68, 69, 88, 110, 114, 131, 169, 207
Massachusetts State Charter, 113, 135
McKinley, Mrs., 95
McKinley, President, 94
Mears, Thomas D., 25
Medford, Mass., 3
Merrimac County Jail, 185
Merrimac River, 18
Mesmerism, 34, 39
Message to The Mother Church for 1900, 152
Message to The Mother Church for 1901
quoted, 37
Message to The Mother Church for 1902
quoted, 26, 92, 123
Methodist Church, 11, 115, 189
Miscellaneous Writings
quoted, 115, 135, 136, 207
Miscellany (See *First Church of Christ, Scientist, and Miscellany, The*)
Montreal, 136
Moore, George H., 117
Moses, George H., 183
Mother Church, The, 5, 6, 70, 100, 104, 116, 117, 119, 122, 124, 138, 142, 145, 147, 148, 149, 152, 160, 164, 166, 168, 183, 194, 205, 207
organized, 113, 114, 135
reorganized, 115, 128
difference between government of The Mother Church and branch churches, 116, 117, 119, 120

Bible and Science and Health ordained as pastor, 143
Mt. Auburn Cemetery, Cambridge, 207
Munroe, Mrs. Mary W., 96
My Husband Gabrilowitsch, 1

N

National Christian Science Association, 85, 131
"Next Friends Suit," 62, 154
New England, 10, 11, 23, 31, 69, 93, 108
New Englander, 10
New England Woman's Press Association, 94
New Hampshire, 18, 22, 26, 28, 30, 39, 93, 110, 115, 150, 154, 177, 179, 180–182, 191, 192
New Hampshire Historical Society, 180
New Hampshire legislature, 18
New Hampshire Patriot, 92
New Hampshire Senate, 165
New Hampshire State Building, 180
New Hampshire State Prison, 186
New Hampton Literary and Biblical Institution, 182
Newspaper Writers' Home, 180
Newton, Mass., 2
New World, 10
New York, 136, 154, 159, 198
New York American, 91
New York Journal, 150
Ninety-first Psalm, 77, 137, 138
North Carolina, 25, 26
North Congregational Meeting House, 11, 17, 117
North Groton, N. H., 31

O

Odd Fellows Hall, East Lynn, 132
Officier d'Académie, 187
Ohio, 3
"Old Home Week," 181
Old Man of the Mountain (poem), 93

T

Texas, 86
Thompson, W. A., 188
Tilton, Abigail (See Baker, Abigail)
Tilton, Alexander H., 27, 28
Tolman, Dr. and Mrs. William H., 187
Tomlinson, Mrs. Elizabeth Cadwell, 57, 160
Tomlinson, Irving C.
attended first service at Chickering Hall, 5
resigned from Universalist Church, 6
became member of class taught by Mrs. Flavia S. Knapp, 5, 6
first visit to original Mother Church, 5
became member of The Mother Church, 6
entered into practice of Christian Science, 6
made member of Bible Lesson Committee, 6
invited to Pleasant View, Independence Day, 1897: 60, 172–175
appointed member of Lecture Board, 6
member of Mrs. Eddy's last class, November, 1898: 6, 85–91
invited to Pleasant View, Dec., 1898: 7
member of Chestnut Hill household, 8, 198–207
invited to become Reader of Concord church, 7, 119
served as Associate Editor of Christian Science periodicals, 101
delivered first lecture ever given by a member of the Board of Lectureship, 132
delivered first lecture in the original edifice of The Mother Church, 133
accompanied Mrs. Eddy to Annual Meeting in Tremont Temple, 1899: 138
appointed by Mrs. Eddy to serve as Committee on Publication for state of N. H., 149, 150
Tomlinson, Mary, 7, 119, 138
Town Hall, Warren, Maine, 130
Tremont Temple, Boston, 138, 139, 141
Tufts College, Medford, 3
Twain, Mark, 1

U

United States, 68, 69, 173, 187, 194, 196
"United States to Great Britain, The," 196
Unitarian Church, 149, 190
Unitarians, 190
Unity of Good, 169
Universalist Church, Arlington, Mass., 3, 6
Universalism, 15, 16
University Press, 103

W

Walker, Hon. Reuben, 115
Warren, Maine, 130
Warren Street, Concord, 179
Washington, D. C., 31, 70
Waterville, Maine, 130
Wentworth, Horace, 41
Wentworth, Lucy, 41
Wentworth, Mrs. Sally, 40, 41
Wilbur, Sibyl, 2
Wilmington, North Carolina, 25, 26
Wilson, John, 103, 104
Wilson, Sol, 80
Woodworth, Mayor, 173
Worcester, Mass., 40

Y

Young Men's Christian Association, 180
Youth and Young Manhood, 97

Z

Zink, M. J. H., 206